Geoff Aigner and **Liz Skelton** are both senior managers, educators and consultants for Social Leadership Australia at The Benevolent Society. They have a rare combination of hands-on experience in senior leadership roles and a deep understanding of change and leadership theory. Geoff is the Director of Social Leadership Australia, adjunct faculty at the Australian Graduate School of Management and the author of *Leadership Beyond Good Intentions*. Liz is Principal Consultant at Social Leadership Australia and brings almost 20 years experience leading social change organisations in Australia and the UK. Together they have led adaptive change initiatives for business, government and community sectors on complex issues such as homelessness, Indigenous leadership and corporate/community engagement.

THE AUSTRALIAN LEADERSHIP PARADOX

WHAT IT TAKES TO LEAD IN THE LUCKY COUNTRY

GEOFF AIGNER AND LIZ SKELTON

ALLEN&UNWIN
SYDNEY • MELBOURNE • AUCKLAND • LONDON

Published by Allen & Unwin in 2013

Copyright © Geoff Aigner and Liz Skelton 2013

All rights reserved. No part of this book may be reproduced or transmitted in any form or by any means, electronic or mechanical, including photocopying, recording or by any information storage and retrieval system, without prior permission in writing from the publisher. The Australian *Copyright Act 1968* (the Act) allows a maximum of one chapter or 10 per cent of this book, whichever is the greater, to be photocopied by any educational institution for its educational purposes provided that the educational institution (or body that administers it) has given a remuneration notice to Copyright Agency Limited (CAL) under the Act.

Allen & Unwin
Sydney, Melbourne, Auckland, London

83 Alexander Street
Crows Nest NSW 2065
Australia
Phone: (61 2) 8425 0100
Fax: (61 2) 9906 2218
Email: info@allenandunwin.com
Web: www.allenandunwin.com

Cataloguing-in-Publication details are available
from the National Library of Australia
www.trove.nla.gov.au

ISBN 978 1 74331 030 4
IBSN 978 1 74331 610 8 (hardback edition)

Illustrations by Ross Carnsew
Set in 13/16 Arno Pro by Bookhouse, Sydney

10 9 8 7 6 5 4 3 2 1

CONTENTS

Acknowledgements ix
Introduction xiii

Part 1 Leadership in Australia—Where are we at?
1 Room to move 3
2 There's no such thing as a 'leader' 14

Part 2 The paradoxes of leadership and authority in Australia
3 The water we swim in 27
4 *Paradox 1*
   Anti-authority and authority-dependent 31
5 *Paradox 2*
   Egalitarian and hierarchical 47
6 *Paradox 3*
   Relational and competitive 60
7 *Paradox 4*
   Battling adversity and living in prosperity 74

Part 3 Shifting practice
8 Leading across difference—The great Australian challenge 87
9 Leading in Australia—The why before the how 99
10 Power, rank and authority 107
11 The leverage of role 125
12 Conflict, growth and innovation 149
13 Doing business with authority—The why 175

14	Doing business differently—The how	189
15	More than surviving	202
16	A new Australian leadership story	210

Endnotes	215
Index	223

ACKNOWLEDGEMENTS

The consulting and leadership development work of Social Leadership Australia (SLA) has provided the experience and testing ground for many of the ideas and practices in this book. Through SLA's students and clients we are fortunate enough to work alongside people from all sectors from all parts of Australia. These are people from all walks of life who are attempting to change their world for the better by exercising leadership. From those at the top of corporations like CEOs in the banking sector, senior bureaucrats in the Australian public service, government ministers and community sector leaders, to those on the frontline like leaders in Indigenous communities, providers of services to the homeless or social entrepreneurs. They have allowed us to develop practical and tested ideas about exercising leadership in a way that carries a positive social and economic intention. We learn from them daily.

We work in collaboration with many skilled teachers and consultants who aim to improve leadership in Australia for the creation of a better nation. They include both our own colleagues and associates at SLA. Their thinking and experiences have contributed greatly to this book.

The experiences and ideas that formed the basis of this book were supported by interviews to test our thinking and provide additional insights. We would like to thank Larissa Behrendt, Tim Costello, Robert Fitzgerald, Gavin Fox-Smith, Geoff Gallop, Greg Hutchinson, Brett Pointing, Simon Sheikh, Ann Sherry, Doug Taylor, Silas Taylor, Simon Terry and Penny Wong. We appreciate your openness, insights and encouragement.

There are a number of people who played a special role in influencing our thinking for this book. The years of learning and debating with Jane Martin have deepened our appreciation and understanding of power and rank and helped us articulate its importance in this book. In our work with Rebekah O'Rourke we were able to test, advance and learn about some of the unique features of leading in Australia. Julie Diamond helped us broaden our thinking and practice on collaboration. Christopher Zinn pointed out and encouraged us to look more closely at the challenge of competition in leadership.

Many skilled and generous people contributed to reviewing all or parts of the manuscript along the way. We were fortunate to receive detailed and page-by-page feedback from our long-term teacher and friend Jane Martin. We received insightful and thoughtful feedback from May Aigner, Rosamund Christie, Maxime Fern, Steve Hawkins, Connie Henson, Anne Hollonds, Michael Johnstone, Shelley Kenigsberg, Diana Renner, Terri Soller, Simon Terry, Dougie Wells, Tracey Young and Christopher Zinn. Thanks to Ross Carnsew for developing illustrations to bring the paradoxes to life.

A special thanks to our publisher Elizabeth Weiss and her team at Allen & Unwin, Sydney, for their support and insight.

Finally, but not at all least, is the support and encouragement of our partners, May Aigner and Dougie Wells, our families and friends who endured not only our absence but also our blockages, confusion and loss of heart as much as our moments of insight, clarity and joy.

For all of you and others, we hope that we have created a piece of work that invites discussion and thought and represents your shared hope for advancing leadership in Australia.

INTRODUCTION

Order! I declare a general warning and I am very serious about it. And I have a sense that members in this chamber are really ignoring how we are perceived from outside. You are now all under a warning!

HON. HARRY JENKINS, SPEAKER
THE HOUSE OF REPRESENTATIVES, AUSTRALIAN PARLIAMENT, JULY 6, 2011[1]

The Australian and global leadership challenges that we face now and in the future will not be solved by our current ways of thinking. The focus on one leader, usually male, with expectations that he will solve our problems, while at the same time maintain our comfortable way of life, is past its use-by date. This expectation is impossible to fulfil and keeps us in a position of dependency. It is an idea about leadership that belongs to a time when there was less complexity and more certainty, when roles and expectations were much clearer and power was deployed in a traditional command and control style.

After more than a decade of consulting and teaching at Social Leadership Australia (SLA) we hear two unmistakeable messages. Firstly, that we face a unique Australian leadership challenge and secondly that the world is calling for new ways to use power well.

We know that a new kind of leadership is needed to match these times, but what exactly are we looking for? This is a global question yet in it lies a uniquely Australian leadership challenge. We cannot ignore what it means to exercise leadership in Australia and what it means to be an Australian. The two are intertwined. This intertwining is what we name in this book as the 'paradoxes of Australian leadership'. We explore how they represent Australia's area of learning and opportunity to make progress.

The purpose of leadership is always and unashamedly about the creation and maintenance of a better world and a more civil society regardless of who is leading and from what sector. It is time to demand that leadership be exercised more effectively in Australia to deliver on this opportunity. This is everyone's problem, and opportunity. How we as Australians, from the prime minister to the business owner, government bureaucrat or grassroots activist, relate to and enact leadership is fundamental to our long-term progress—not just economically, but as citizens.

The last 50 years has seen tremendous material growth in Australia and by global standards the creation of a well-functioning democracy. Australians have freedom, relative prosperity and the power to make choices. We have peace, the advantage of distance and relatively little cultural baggage. We could wait for others to lead, locally or globally, or we could do it better ourselves. It is an opportunity for us as individual Australians doing our daily work and for the country as a whole. This opportunity is for all Australians regardless of culture, race, gender, level, sector and location.

There are times when the only pragmatic course is to be visionary.[2]

INTRODUCTION

This book is an ambitious and naive venture. It aims to shift the thinking and practice of leadership in Australia, by Australians—for all Australians. To do this we need to understand more fully who we are, where we are, how we got here and what might transform our leadership.

These are the questions we need to ask if we are to shift our thinking and practice of leadership:

- What does leadership look like in Australia?
- How did we get here?
- What's the opportunity before us at this stage in our development as a nation?
- What would make a difference in how we all operate so that leadership can improve in every sector?

The answers to these questions may go some way to answer the dissatisfaction with, and confusion about, leadership in Australia. In early discussions about writing this book, we received a chorus of approval and encouragement from almost everyone we met. 'Yes. You need to write about *that*!' This was consistent, whether we were talking to people in the government or business, academia or community, young or old, country or city, black or white, and men and women. There seems to be a general agreement that things need to shift in how we take up the roles of leadership.

But to what? This question generates less consistent responses or a perplexed silence. We seem to know what we don't want and don't like. But when it comes to leadership, we find it hard to articulate, let alone agree on, what we *do* want. We also haven't thought too much about how we got to this point in terms of leadership or how we could participate in making it different.

Without a clear idea about what we want from leadership, we struggle to make progress on fundamental changes for the future. We ignore the impact of the way we exercise leadership and are drawn to the short term, negative and divisive. This manifests in a culture of complaint about leadership which is incongruent with how the world sees us and how we see ourselves. Australia remains an optimistic and solutions-oriented country. How do we reconcile a generally poor report card on leadership with one of the highest standards of living in the world, a safe and stable democracy in a unique and beautiful landscape? Are we channelling all of our pessimism and cynicism into one place—leadership?

Or does this complaint and dissatisfaction relate to our unsatisfied hopes and dreams? We saw this hope awakened in the election campaign for former prime minister Kevin Rudd in 2007. The 'Kevin 07' campaign ignited an optimism and hope that many reported they had not felt for years. With the benefit of hindsight we can see that it was doomed to wane when the reality of enacting change emerged. Whilst this story had a more dramatic and rapid end than usual, the waxing and waning on leadership is predictable.

We can wait for the next saviour and suffer the inevitable disappointment when our expectations fail us. Alternatively, we can start thinking differently about what leadership means and what we want from our leaders and ourselves.

Hope for purposeful leadership

We are often asked by our course participants and clients to give Australian examples of good leadership. When we look 'up' at those in formal positions of power and 'out' to those who are led—it is not an inspiring picture. That is not to say that useful leadership is not being exercised in Australia. It is, but often in unexpected and less visible places in communities, organisations and systems.

Effective leadership is characterised by actions that have positive impacts beyond ourselves. It is not management, entrepreneurism or dictatorship. It involves using our privilege and power to connect with others to create progress for the whole of the country, not just one part of it. It enables people to understand and solve their own problems. This means that leadership always embodies a higher dream and purpose that things are left better than we found them—more resilient communities, sustainable organisations and people who are willing to step up and take over when we are gone. This kind of leadership needs to extend across business, government and the community sectors. It is not confined to any one place, profession or level.

To shift the thinking and practice of leadership in Australia is an ambitious goal. It won't happen through some new government policy or dazzling leadership model from overseas or the arrival of a political saviour. Rather it relies on each of us understanding what leadership really means for us, for the future we seek and how we use what resources we have differently. It is inevitably and inextricably linked to exploring the kind of life we want to live and the world we want to live in.

Who else other than us as Australians has the opportunity to ask these questions and indeed answer them? Who else has the natural resources and high national social and political stability? And who else is as unencumbered by the expectations that constrain larger powers?

Like never before in our history, our high privilege is matched only by a lack of a clear and compelling vision for the future: something to *lead towards*. One could argue that the complaint and negativity about leadership in Australia today is largely a function of failing to sense and create the future we want. To paraphrase an old Zen proverb: *As long as we look obsessively at ourselves we find problems. When we look outwards we find useful things to do.*

We have the power to make progress and we have the opportunity to take responsibility for that power. The exercise of power with responsibility gives rise to the opportunity for both wisdom and compassion. As Geoff Gallop, former premier of Western Australia, reminds us:

> Accept your responsibilities and really care for their application. Always take the debate to another level. The responsibility of leaders in all aspects of life is to keep raising the debate to a higher level, always thinking about the bigger picture and reflecting that in all you say and do.

This attitude and practice can provide the opportunity for growth in us as individuals and foster the potential in our organisations and societies.

It's time to stop accepting anything less in our ideas and practice of leadership.

A world dream or more of the same?

This is not just an Australian challenge. There is a world dream or hope for better leadership. Every day there are examples from around the world that show this hope for a new way of leading. Perhaps this hope has always been there.

> There was a moment in Tahrir [during the protests in Cairo in 2011 which eventually saw Egyptian President Mubarak fall],

early on, when sitting on a low wall I watched two young men walking towards me, deep in conversation. One was saying: 'The parliamentary system will be better for us because we need to break away from the cult of the leader,' and the other interrupted: 'But the "leader" doesn't have to be a dictator; he could be a useful . . .'[3]

Recent years have seen this hope matched by a concentrated shift in the existing power structures and fierce, open challenges to what those in authority and power should be doing. Social media and the impact of Wikileaks have allowed large numbers of people to gain information and exchange ideas. How those with power treat their constituents, how people seek change or stability (often at the same time) and how we tackle problems and difficulties is visible around the world as they happen:

- In Tunisia a wave of protests is sparked by the death of a young vegetable vendor, Mohammed Bouazizi, in December 2010. In an act of desperation Bouazizi set fire to himself after officials stopped him selling vegetables without permission. The ensuing 'jasmine revolution' led to the overthrow in January 2011 of Zine el Abidine Ben Ali, president of 23 years.
- In 2011 in Egypt, inspired by events in Tunisia, a groundswell of protest against the ruling government sees Hosni Mubarak fall from power after 30 years as president, (hopefully) ending decades of dictatorial rule and corruption.
- In the Ivory Coast, President Laurent Gbagbo's refusal to step down after Alassane Ouattara won the 2010 election reignited a civil war that claimed more than 1000 lives and uprooted a million people. He is eventually captured in April 2011 by opposition forces and faces trial in The Hague.

- In Japan in March 2011, 30 000 people die or go missing following an earthquake and ensuing tsunami. The tsunami precipitated the world's worst nuclear disaster in a quarter of a century. At the centre of the nuclear crisis was the reactor's owner, TEPCO. Fierce criticism was levelled at the company and its old-style 'salaryman' management for its slow response and lack of transparency. As billions were wiped off the company's share value, the 66-year-old President Masataka Shimizu disappeared from public view for more than two weeks.
- In Libya opposition forces seek to extract the 69-year-old Muammar Gaddafi from power after 41 years as self-declared 'King of Kings'. He is eventually overthrown and summarily executed in 2011.

One could say that social media has emboldened people, created transparency and contributed to a global call for change. There is talk about a global 'democratisation of leadership': people authorising themselves in new ways through social media and global grassroots advocacy.

Maybe there is a new wave of social change coming and the problems are just those of old, stubborn megalomaniac men who find it hard to change and give up power. This hope, while held widely, is perhaps too simple an idea. Unfortunately, history has shown that new tyrants with hope, glory and expectation very quickly fill the shoes of the old ones. Muammar Gaddafi, Idi Amin and Robert Mugabe were all revolutionaries, too.

What happens when the old, stubborn and selfish have been pushed aside? What arises to take their place? Will it be useful and beneficial to society, organisations and government? Or will it be more of the same?

Do we want more of the same?

What is stuck can become unstuck

Australians are seeking a more useful form of leadership: one that moves away from the traditional ideas of leadership that characterise the current debate. First of all we need to be aware of what we have. Through our work in SLA we often engage with significantly powerful people. The most striking thing we notice is how little opportunity they have to gain awareness of their power, purpose and role, and even less opportunity to learn how to do something different with it. This is a challenge for all of us who have some power and want to use it responsibly.

This book is about hope and practical steps to make change. Thankfully, it is *not* about problems nor is it a brand new set of tools and techniques that claim to revolutionise the leadership landscape. We don't believe there are any new models or tools that can save us. There is already much wisdom in the world. We need to continue to find new and fresh ways to access it.

We offer an alternative lens on what is happening and what could happen in the Australian leadership context. We bring together theory, processes and practices that challenge the idea that leaders must be superhuman, and we show how flaws, doubts and difficulties contain the seeds of opportunity. Our aim is to increase the awareness needed for useful and effective leadership to be practised and to provide ideas on how to bring fluidity to stuck situations.

The focus on the practice of leadership provides a transition to a lighter and more useful form of leading both for ourselves and those around us. It is also a work in progress. Just like leadership in Australia.

> ... but there are signs that the children of this generation may prove wiser either than the children of God or the children of

light. The Aborigines have called on white people to redress an ancient wrong: the Aborigines have rediscovered the source of their strength in their relationship with the land and the spirit of the place ... Australians have liberated themselves from the fate of being second-rate Europeans. Australians have begun to contribute to the never-ending conversation of humanity on the meaning of life, and the means of wisdom and understanding ... Now is the time for the life-affirmers and the enlargers to show whether they have anything to say, whether they have any food for the great hungers of humanity.[4]

Australia has the power to choose a story in which we absolve ourselves of responsibility to lead while blaming those who do. We also have the power to choose a different story: one in which we use even the worst and most difficult circumstances to create learning and growth in our world. This requires us to get specific about the deeper purpose and practice of effective leadership. That means we, as Australians, can become the storyteller.

This book is unashamedly trying to foster a new leadership story, one that is more useful for all of us—wherever we are and whatever we are doing.

Who we are

Geoff and I work for Social Leadership Australia, a social enterprise at The Benevolent Society, Australia's oldest independent charity established in 1813. SLA was created to develop better leadership for a better Australia. It runs its own leadership programs, consults to organisations, advocates for a new form of leadership and instigates initiatives on some of our most complex leadership challenges. We work with leaders in the business, government and community sectors to develop better leadership to make progress on our most pressing social and economic leadership challenges.

Geoff is a second-generation Australian and I am an Australian citizen, originally from Scotland. We believe it is important to have a man and woman writing this book, as well as the mix of sector, cultural and life experiences we each bring. We do not claim to represent Australia in all of its diversity, culture, race and geography.

We know from our work that it is almost impossible to teach leadership if you have not had direct experience of it in roles of authority. We draw extensively on our own experiences in these roles to inform our daily work and the material in this book. We also draw on the experiences and learnings from the thousands of Australians we have worked with who are exercising leadership in their organisations and communities on a daily basis. Our purpose is to advance leadership because we believe in the social, economic and psychological development of Australia.

An acknowledgement of where we need to learn

In our work advancing Australian leadership, we affirm the need to find ways for Indigenous and non-Indigenous people to work together and learn from each other. Ultimately, we believe leading *together* is core to Australia's progress as well as to being able to congruently own its leadership role in the world.

Leadership in Australia contains all the stories and influences from those leaders who have preceded us. Starting with the original Indigenous tribal leaders, to those who colonised Australia, established the penal settlements, led the convicts and settlers in developing the cities and farming land, and those who were transported. The story continues today with those who migrated or fled here to build a better life. But that is only a very small part of the story.

We are conscious that as white Australians we are drawing mostly on the story of the country's most recent history over the last 200 years. We are aware that the knowledge and teachings from Indigenous culture impact Australian life and that whilst we have, under their supervision, developed some measure of cultural competency, much of this is still outside of our understanding. The wisdom of Indigenous leadership and it's potential to shape Australia's future is still largely untapped. Leveraging this wisdom may assist black and white Australians to create a new narrative for leading—one where we lead together. As this potential emerges, we are using this incomplete knowledge and expertise to try to progress leadership in Australia. While imperfect, we believe that in attempting to lead you cannot wait to have all the information you need, you still have to keep trying to move forward. That is our motivation to write this book.

PART 1

LEADERSHIP IN AUSTRALIA— WHERE ARE WE AT?

CHAPTER 1

ROOM TO MOVE

The extraordinary thing is that Australia has never looked more appealing to the rest of the world . . . The 2010 [federal election] campaign is the sound of a nation needlessly fracturing.
GEORGE MEGALOGANIS, *QUARTERLY ESSAY 40*, 2011[1]

What's happening in Australian leadership?

What impression might an outsider arriving for the first time in Australia make of leadership if they tuned into the public discourse, media commentary and dinner table conversations? What would they make of the challenges we face and how those challenges are being met? How might they view the role of those leading versus those who are being led?

It might seem that 'bagging' those in positions of authority was some kind of national sport: one that has no boundaries—government, business and community; city or country; young or old; men and women; and black and white. They could be forgiven for thinking that Australian leadership is in a precarious state

and that we face a real and urgent leadership crisis—not just politically, but also in our organisations and communities.

The complaint is not just about politicians. How many times have you been with a group of people and participated in a conversation complaining about those in power? It could be about the 'stupid' decisions they make or about an absence of leadership. *If only they could just . . . (insert opinion here).* We can all be dinner table complainers and leadership is an easy target. And the answer? Usually a new leader—someone, somewhere, who can fix the problems we face. In an episode of *Mornings* on 774 ABC, Melbourne, the host Jon Faine asked, 'Since when did whingeing become a defining characteristic and an inseparable part of the over-invoked great Aussie spirit?'[2]

At a dinner party Liz found herself joining in with the predictable complaining about the latest political issue. As she looked around the table she realised how much power everyone had. All held positions of authority and power in either the corporate, community or government sector. Yet it was difficult for individuals in the group, including her, to acknowledge their power or their part in the problem. She also observed how much energy the dynamic of complaining can generate. It started to feed itself, rising in intensity, triggering wave after wave of complaint.

This is not a uniquely Australian phenomenon nor is it necessarily a problem in itself. Cynicism, ridicule and criticism of those in positions of power is as old as humankind, whether it is happening openly or behind closed doors. Even in the most authoritarian and totalitarian regimes, people have found vent for their frustrations discreetly in trusted circles. The jokes often highlight the gap between reality as it is experienced by the public, and the ideology or propaganda coming from those in authority. These jokes, or sarcastic barbs, emerge in any organisation or community. They are a great barometer of the gap between the ideas being put forward and the sentiment of those who are supposed to implement them.

It is one of the privileges of democracy that we can complain and voice our opinions. But have we forgotten where we live? Are things really so bad for us all? Surely the 'lucky country' doesn't have such poor leadership. Or does it?

This is a question that could be asked in any developed country with a free press and functioning protections for citizens and labour. A year out from the 2012 American presidential election, a study by Pew Research found that 'negative assessments of President Obama outweighed positive by a ratio of almost 4 to 1'.[3]

It seems that when the increasingly shorter, honeymoon period is over for a new leader, we revert to a pattern of dissatisfaction with the leader's performance. Similarly, in the same time period, the Pew research found Republican primary candidates got comparatively much more positive coverage because they were only being judged on their promises rather than the realities of what they implemented. Candidates always fare better than incumbents in perceptions of leadership.

The antipathy between followers and leaders is not a one-way street.[4] Those in leadership roles also complain about the lack of engagement in leadership issues from ordinary people, community members or employees. This has been perpetuated and exaggerated by the 'consumerisation of followers'. In politics there are endless polls and voter research. In our communities, governments conduct numerous community 'consultations'. And in our organisations we are faced with an increasingly advanced and growing set of measurements such as 360-degree feedback tools, culture assessments and organisation engagement measures. All of these measurements and feedback mechanisms can turn employees and citizens into customers, drained of agency,[5] especially when they participate in a process of having their voice heard yet see nothing change as a result.

Complaining and critique is inevitable. The freedom to comment on the system is a sign of a healthy democracy and an unavoidable human reaction to power. In some ways it can be an idle and satisfying pastime. The question is whether it dominates our relationship to leadership. Does it help us make progress?

The Wizard of (not just) Oz

> ... and you wondered if Australians were unique in thinking that they lived in the best country and were the best people in the world, and yet were governed by the worst people in the worst possible way.[6]

The complaint and critique are signals of a fantasy about leadership that is not limited to Australia. It is a global hope, or even collusion, about leadership. We hope that our problems will be solved by a mythical figure or that we will be that figure ourselves. We often call this figure the 'leader'. As in the story of the *Wizard of Oz*, there is a belief about a man in the Emerald City with powers to solve all of our problems with little work from us.

This is a fantasy that surrounds us daily. It is often accompanied by the following phrases:

- 'What we need is some leadership here.'
- 'We need someone to show leadership.'
- 'We need *real* leadership here!'

We want someone to be strong and take control. We want someone who can do the hard work and relieve the confusion, conflict or pain. We may find ourselves trying to fulfil that fantasy ourselves. There is nothing malicious in this fantasy. We are brought up to look to our authority figures for answers and relief when things are difficult.

We want our leaders to make change that improves things for us, not change where we may have to give up anything or do things differently. In addition, we expect our leaders to be flawless role models with all the answers, yet be vulnerable and human at the same time.

There's nothing wrong with trying to fulfil others' expectations. Parents, managers and political leaders need to fulfil their functions of providing direction, offering protection and maintaining order.[7] These functions are crucial to maintain our daily lives. However, the fantasy fails us when there is no quick fix, when we are required to do some of the work ourselves or undergo some loss or difficulty. When our leaders inevitably fail these ideals and expectations we can be savage in cutting them down and we then revert back to complaining and critiquing.

This makes us easily seduced by new leaders. A new CEO, politician or prime minister builds our hopes up again that it will be different and better than the last time. Like looking behind the green curtain in the *Wizard of Oz*, we soon find that the wizard is just a normal person operating levers and speaking into a microphone. This reality is difficult to bear and it is usually easier to seek a new wizard to fulfil the fantasy than face the reality ourselves. This is a cyclical process.

Effective leadership can then seem unattainable. Our idea of leadership may be so ambitious that we can justify to ourselves that we could never do it. When we see the examples of people who have devoted their entire lives to the cause, suffered extreme hardship and sacrifice, it's no wonder that many people say it's not for them. 'I'm no Mandela or Gandhi.' We have this idea that for leadership to truly work, it requires us to be superhuman, omnipotent or, even worse, a martyr. Some of this is hard-wired. Many of the stories and fables that we grew up with extol the leader as superhuman:

> He must loan himself for the benefit of society or an organisation. Great leaders who create radical changes are supposed to totally relinquish their personality and be absorbed by their role. The ultimate leaders are those who relinquished their private life in favour of society's needs.[8]

We shouldn't be surprised then by the number of people working really hard, exercising leadership daily in their organisations, who do not dare call themselves 'leaders'. That's because the world implies an ideal no-one can ever really measure up to. The perpetuation of this fantasy around leadership provides a ready escape route out of action and responsibility.

However, there is also a noble value in the fantasy. Our yearning for progress is a very human desire. The corollary of our fantasy is our very real fear that perhaps no-one has the answer to how we make progress, and that our leaders are as flawed as us. What we might really risk losing is our fantasy about leadership.

So can Australians lead?

> The elements of loyalty . . . competitiveness, ambition and struggle that are not allowed precise expression in non-sporting life (although they exist in disguise) are stated precisely in sport.[9]

Where is it okay to exercise leadership in Australia?

Where is it acceptable to own our power and take pride in achievement? To stand out?

To not require a crisis to do something different?

To take initiative and achieve?

Donald Horne, among several other commentators on Australian life, observed that sport is one domain where we can safely allow our dreams to come to life. In sport we can back ourselves, stand out from the crowd and be powerful. We can applaud others' achievements and expect a high moral standard. We expect sportspeople to fulfil their roles and achieve, and we don't tolerate poor performance, even from 'a mate'. We respect the need for authority, hierarchy and leadership at the right time.

In sport we find it easier to see beyond the complaint and get a glimpse into what we as Australians dream about. If sporting achievement is a metaphor for our dreams about leadership and power, clearly we like to stand out in the world. We like to work together and respect and accept our power. We enjoy and celebrate skill and achievement. We like to win. We are not values-neutral and in this realm that's okay.

But if we can't take this dream beyond sport, we can easily end up being spectators. In Australia there are many spectators of leadership and it doesn't look like such a great game to watch. Yet if we don't leave the stands, who will lead?

Who do we leave leadership to (when we don't leave the stands)?

In 2011, the Murdoch media empire became embroiled in a protracted scandal involving primarily the *News of the World* newspaper published by News International in the UK. Employees of the organisation were accused of phone and computer hacking (including police bribery) to enhance their reporting not only of politicians, the royal family and celebrities, but also of murdered schoolgirl Milly Dowler, relatives of British soldiers killed in action, and victims of the 7/7 London bombings. The stories led to a public enquiry in Britain, FBI investigations in the United States, and a string of arrests and resignations in both News Limited and the police. The *News of the World* closed after 168 years of operation.

This example gives us an opportunity to examine the purpose and use of power. In particular it shows what can happen when we don't take responsibility for leading and leadership—when we spectate.

As the story began to unfold in July 2011, Rupert Murdoch, Chairman and Chief Executive of News Corporation, flew into London to deal with the fallout. Outside his apartment he was asked by reporters what his 'number one priority' was. He pointed to the (then) Chief Executive of News International, Rebekah Brooks, and said, 'This one.'

This is a telling moment in the use of power. It is mirrored in many other instances in Australian organisational, political and community life. What does this moment communicate to other stakeholders such as the bereaved families whose deceased loved ones' phones had been hacked by the *News* reporters? Or customers, shareholders and employees? With people losing jobs and shareholders facing a slide of over 10 per cent in share value, why is the wellbeing of reportedly one of the most powerful women in the UK a 'number one priority'?

Brooks subsequently 'resigned' and the non-Murdoch press, the public and newly emboldened politicians had a field day demonising Murdoch and his clan. There was gleeful and widespread railing at the nepotism and *News of the World*'s greed and lack of ethics. The belated apology to families made by Murdoch a few weeks later was seen as nothing more than a cynical media exercise. And perhaps rightly so.

It is nonetheless wise to be cautious when we find ourselves enjoying (too much) the failings of those with power and taking pleasure in their downfall. As Greg Hutchinson, Director of the Australian Charities Fund and Goodstart Early Learning Centres, reflects:

> We celebrate failures of leadership too often, whether in politics, business or essential services. By focusing on failure we undermine trust in these roles. In the process we discourage those who might responsibly exercise leadership.

There is never a shortage of flawed and seemingly ethics-free leaders and organisations in the world and Australia has had its share, too. There is an old adage, 'If you can't be a good example, at least be a terrible warning.' We have had many warnings about what it looks like when those with power don't own or take responsibility for their impact on all of society, rather than just the chosen few.

Power is an easy target upon which to project our shortcomings. Yet, we can all be selfish, nepotistic and short-sighted. All of us can think of ourselves first at the expense of others. We hope that most of the time our better selves win—sometimes this doesn't happen. In leading, it can feel like we are in a battle between what's good for us as individuals and what's good for the whole. However, this idea of a trade-off between the whole and self is flawed. Exercising leadership that is good for society invariably is good for the self. When citizens, leaders, parents, bosses or employees are taking responsibility for their power and using it carefully, all of society can benefit.

While we may have a dream and hope about leadership, that is not enough on its own. We need to start making it a reality. If we don't, we end up in the cycle of complaint that feeds itself. We stay in a place of being a passive observer as opposed to a potential participant. If we spent the same amount of energy owning our ability to influence change as we spend complaining about leadership, we might find that we already have significant *room to move* in Australia. As we discover in 'The Wizard of Oz':

> The three decide to accompany Dorothy in hopes that the Wizard will also fulfil their desires, although they demonstrate that they already have the qualities they believe they lack.[10]

We have room to move

Some of our room to move lies in the space and distance of our geography. One could say that the creation of modern Australia was founded on a need for space—specifically a space to send

British convicts. As the overflow of jailed British prisoners spilled over into the temporary accommodation of old hulks on the Thames, Australia provided the required space. The British outsourced their problems to an area that was conveniently out of sight and mind—the other side of the planet.

This space and distance, while providing temporarily relief for a colonial power (but not the same for the local Indigenous population), was in many ways more a problem than a blessing for the early settlers. Australia was far from the motherland. It was far from what was considered civilisation and far from protection in an adverse and remote landscape. Yet, what began as a curse has in many ways become a blessing.

Space has become one of the great opportunities in a shrinking and increasingly resource-poor world. Beyond the material advantage and perhaps because of it, our space provides the potential to think freely and be creative. Our distance from many fixed traditions and norms provides an opportunity to build what is required both now and for the future. We are freer than most to break from the past and not just continue its trajectory. This space is an opportunity as long as we see it as a privilege and not a right. As a right it dulls our thinking and lessens the need to bring useful and skilful leadership into play.

But what does it mean to lead usefully anyway?

CHAPTER 2

THERE'S NO SUCH THING AS A 'LEADER'

Of all of our political expectations none is more remarkable or unfair than our insistence that our prime minister govern for all of us. We expect him to know what we, in all our myriad manifestations as citizens, are feeling—even when our feelings are at odds with what an equal number of our fellow citizens are feeling, or are inflamed beyond reason by false and misleading information, or the lack of information, or the comforts and irritations we receive from talkback radio hosts. We expect him to find wisdom in our perceptions, however false and ill-informed our perceptions may be. We expect him to know what we are needing; what we are going through; what we are hoping for; what we are uncertain about and sensitive to. We expect him to share and give voice to our aspirations. We demand that he barrack for us and our children against our enemies, though they may be more necessitous than ourselves. We expect him to listen to us and yet to lead us; to obey our will and yet be leader enough to have a will of his own; to reflect our view and yet project his vision. It's a tall order, but one a prime minister had better be seen to obey.[1]

DON WATSON

This quote illustrates the range of projections we have on all those in the role of authority, not just the prime minister. The role of authority is one of the least known and most commonly misunderstood roles in leadership. Yet, when people who want to lead understand their purpose, their power and what's required of the role of authority, the impact they can have is significant. What often gets in the way is a fundamental confusion about what is commonly mistaken for leadership—authority.

The following chapters explore a number of hypotheses about the landscape of Australian leadership. The role and function of authority is central to these hypotheses. So firstly we map out the distinctions between leadership and authority and when each of these are called for. In doing so, we draw primarily on the model of adaptive leadership from Ronald Heifetz and Marty Linsky at the Harvard Kennedy School as we find this to be the most useful way to understand the distinctions. It makes the role of authority clear and if or where exercising leadership is required.

What is authority?

So what is authority and how is it different to leadership? Every system needs to have clear authority to enable it to work well. Authority is a role with a clear mandate and expectations to deliver the core functions required for a system's survival. These are the functions of direction, protection and order. To understand these functions more deeply, let's start with the first system we are involved in—the family:

- Direction—If we are lucky we have parents or guardians who can give us enough direction through life to support our survival and growth. First of all they direct us in where to get food,

they send us to school, provide advice and help us understand the outside world. This supports us in navigating an unknown future and complex systems. This direction is so important some of these functions are taken out of parents' hands and managed by a higher authority. For example, compulsory school education is enforced and managed by the state.
- Protection—When we are safe and loved we are able to develop and grow as human beings. Particularly in the very early stages of life, we learn how to engage with the rest of the world while being protected by our parents. This takes many forms—from providing a roof over our heads, to warning and educating us about dangers in the outside world. As we move out into other systems, this authority is invested in other people such as teachers, police and employers.
- Order—When they are functioning well, families provide some structure and discipline to our lives. As children, our parents ensured we got up in the morning, ate at certain times of the day and learnt routines that prepare us for succeeding in the structured environments of our schools, social networks and workplaces.

Authority plays a key role in ensuring the smooth functioning of all the systems with which we engage and access: home, school, commercial, leisure and civic. Indeed, many of the problems we face in community and organisational life stem from a lack of authority. Abdication, abuse or absence of authority has long-lasting and serious consequences. When those in authority don't fulfil their functions, we end up with neglected children in families or corruption in organisations.

Authority works at its best when the system is experiencing little change or disruption. The role of authority does not necessarily *lead* through this time. When authority fulfils its functions of providing direction, protection and order, it enables the status quo to operate. Children are fed, buses run on time, schools are open, we have law and order, and our systems are able to function. If we only focused on improving how the role of authority is taken up, we could go a long way towards improving our communities, government and organisations. We call this management. It's good management when it works well but it's not leadership. To understand when leadership is required, we need to make the distinction between technical and adaptive challenges.[2]

Technical challenges

The vast majority of work in any system is technical. This is the routine work that happens every day and that makes our societies and economies function:[3] such as responding to customer enquiries, running a mining operation or transport system, or delivering government services. We know how to do these things or have access to the experts who can. Technical challenges call for a response from our existing repertoire of experiences, skills and processes. If the challenges are known to us; it doesn't mean they are easy to solve, they can be quite complicated—but we can access what we know or what we can readily find out.

A society's ability to respond to technical challenges is fundamental to its survival. It requires not only know-how and resources but also a functioning system of authority. As an advanced and stable nation Australia is relatively effective at dealing with most technical challenges. Authority works well here almost all of the time. This can be seen equally in both our response to crisis as well as the management of the routine of modern life. We walk out onto the streets at night and there are lights on, there is water in our taps and the ATM has cash. In a crisis we have teams of highly trained police, medical professionals and disaster relief specialists ready to spring into action. We are surrounded, luckily, by evidence of our ability to deal with technical challenges and the people we authorise to deal with these are adept at responding to them. *These kinds of challenges don't require us to change—they require us to respond.*

Our adeptness at doing technical work is testament to the integrity and skill of Australians in the role and function of authority. Authority provides the required direction, protection and order to make our daily lives functional, whether it's in the context of a family or a multinational organisation. This enables society to operate well, until our environment changes around us or we face a different type of threat or opportunity. Then we may have an adaptive challenge on our hands.

Adaptive challenges

Adaptive challenges are quite different to technical challenges, although on the surface they may look the same. These types of challenges require an adaptation from the system. Or, in other words, they require the whole system to learn. They may be beyond the system's ability to respond in the moment because these problems (and opportunities) by their nature:

- Can be difficult to understand or predict (e.g. the global financial crisis)
- Have longer time horizons for both causes and effects (e.g. climate change)
- Include differences in values and assumptions from those involved (e.g. Australia's response to refugee arrivals).

The normal ways of operating that enabled the system to work well are usually not sufficient to deal with the new adaptive challenge. Ann Sherry, CEO of Carnival Australia, reflected on how this has been playing out in Australia:

> We are having to think more expansively about leadership in a more complex environment. You can see by the churn of CEOs, there have been a lot of people who were good technicians, or had been around for a long time. People have realised that doing the same stuff doesn't get you there, doing it with the same people doesn't get you there. You get shown up really only when the market moves and you don't see it or you're not ready for it.

We see these challenges in organisational life all the time where circumstances change and our people, systems, processes and culture struggle to adapt quickly enough to compete or respond in the new environment. Systems usually respond as if the problem is a technical one—misdiagnosing the challenge and applying a known solution to the problem. This usually means the problem will remain and often get worse even though we may believe we have addressed it.

The Australian media sector is a case in point of a system that has had to undertake significant adaptation. Its core processes and ways of working remained the same whilst gradually, over a number of years, the environment it operates in has shifted. The sector has struggled to deal with the challenges of shifting media platforms, the changing role of journalists and a dramatic shift in the business model for classifieds. It wasn't until revenue started to decline rapidly that those in positions of authority began to take notice and adapt to its new reality.

For any system going through adaptation, the change may mean giving up ways of doing things which have benefited the system in the past. This is difficult to accept when the pay-offs are not immediately obvious or perhaps not there at all in the short term. Just like it is in nature, organisations either adapt or die out. The change, if lasting and effective, is rarely fast or dramatic. Cataclysmic change is rare.

In fact usually change is actually much more conservative, despite what we hope or fear. Adaptive change feels radical because what is changing is often deeply important to us.

If we think about some of the more complex adaptive challenges we face in Australia—for example, climate change, reconciliation between black and white Australia, tax reform or our national response to asylum-seekers—there is very little that will substantially change. Almost everything will stay the same—language, landscape, Australian values and norms, culture and traditions, distribution of wealth and status.

One of the most divisive issues in Australia's recent history, the introduction of carbon pricing, saw a dramatic and heated response to a very marginal change. The pricing was introduced in 2012 as a staged process to shift towards a trading scheme where the market sets the price of carbon. It established elaborate compensation schemes to ensure that very few Australians were impacted, particularly those earning less than $70 000 per annum. In the lead-up to the introduction of the pricing, the political fallout for the Gillard government, scare-mongering and confusion were probably without precedent in most people's memories. So what was all the fuss? This response was in itself a highly conservative response to a complex adaptive challenge—the larger issue of climate change.

It is easy to say that it was all political gamesmanship in a quest for power. But there's more to it than that. Changes such as these represent the core of any adaptive challenge in the human context because we are being asked to contemplate:

- How we live
- What we value and
- How much it may cost.

The carbon-pricing challenge was a relatively small change in the bigger scheme of the future of Australian life—for most people it has been quickly forgotten. But the issue was a hard and risky one for the Gillard government to sustain. This is because the broader challenge that we were being engaged in—climate change—does not have readily apparent solutions. The problem is not easily understood or agreed on, let alone the required responses. This makes the job of those in authority (government) difficult because they are unable to fulfil the expectation of others that they will just fix the problem—as they can with technical challenges. The work of adaptive leadership is to engage Australia, with its diversity of values and interests, in what we are willing to give up and what needs to be retained. That's where the work begins.

What does leadership look like?

The work of leadership is to mobilise people to face their new realities and solve their own problems. It 'is in helping systems tackle problems which do not have ready-made answers and will inevitably mean some kind of difficulty or loss in the short term'.[4] This can take many forms. It can be a doctor's role in helping a patient face and deal with a life-threatening health issue where they may need to change their lifestyle and habits. Or an organisational leader trying to understand and address continued employee disengagement. In both these cases a simple pill or another restructure by those in charge is unlikely to fix the problem. What's required is for those in authority to help the system understand the nature of the challenge and to mobilise the system to respond. This is because the system (either as individuals or a whole group) will need to adapt. And adaptation requires loss as much as it involves gain. If there were no loss, the change would have happened already.

It is in the face of adaptive challenges that we hear the cry for leadership. What this usually means is that we are looking for those with authority to just fix the problem for us. Unfortunately, in an adaptive challenge, authority can't just implement a ready-made solution. Even if the solutions were known it may not be one that enough people will accept, and the problem requires everyone including authority to adapt.

So there's no such thing as a leader?

This brings us to the word 'leader', which represents the confusion best. This title is inevitably given to those in a system with a role of authority—formal or informal. It is a role onto which we project an expectation that all, or at least many of, our problems will be solved. And because it's a noun and not a verb it is misleading. We begin to think that being a leader is something we are and leadership is something we have, as opposed to something we do. When we start to think about leadership as an activity as opposed to a position, we can begin to make progress.

These distinctions are important because we tend to superimpose our expectations of authority and ideas of what we think needs to be done onto the exercising of leadership. In reality they are separate roles and require different responses. We need to own our authority first before we can exercise any leadership. By seeing the difference between authority and leadership, we are able to see what role we may be playing in our system's adaptation and just how much room we have to make a difference.

PART 2

THE PARADOXES OF LEADERSHIP AND AUTHORITY IN AUSTRALIA

CHAPTER 3

THE WATER WE SWIM IN

I think people in Australia have this view that there are great leaders. I have become more convinced that leadership is contextual to time, place, history, culture, role and responsibility.

ROBERT FITZGERALD, COMMISSIONER,
AUSTRALIAN PRODUCTIVITY COMMISSION

The search for a central leadership figure is a common theme—in politics, religion, community and business life. The need for a figure who can guide, protect and provide us with answers is a recurrent global leadership dynamic. This is the fantasy of leadership.[1] We project our power and agency as well as our needs onto this idealised figure. When the fantasy bubble bursts due to some misdemeanour or inability to deliver the ideal, we blame the person for being less than perfect and no more than human.

The strength of this fantasy may be different depending on the time and place. It may be expressed in different ways—but it will always be there. Another dominant element of leadership across culture and geography is the prevalence of male leaders and masculine leadership models—although it is slowly shifting.

Some common elements in leadership across the planet have more to do with being human and the development of the human race than our specific cultural identities and nationalities. Additionally, every country faces its own unique leadership challenges in their environment and their responses, as well as how they exercise leadership.

This part of the book examines some of the most prevalent leadership dynamics in the Australian context. These are important to understand because it is impossible to exercise leadership independent of our context. This is not meant to be an answer to, and explanation of, everything that happens in leadership in Australia. Rather it gives us a compass for understanding what we take for granted in Australian leadership and a framework for examining why this might be happening.

An Indigenous elder in the Illawarra region of New South Wales points out that if you really know your country you can paint its every feature true to how it appears from an aerial view. This means that you can read the landscape and see which way to go without running out of water. If we better understand the leadership landscape in which we are operating, we can identify what we need and what we can use to make progress. We can even predict in advance what might get in the way.

We begin with trying to understand how we got to this point in the history of Australian leadership. We do this by examining the landscape and the forces that have influenced how we interact with leadership roles in Australia. Let's start this at the level of the individual. Geoff would like to use his power more responsibly and authentically but sometimes struggles to own his authority. His personal history may provide some clues. As a dark-skinned child of immigrants where his school environment favoured the physically strong and blond, where authority figures were at best uncaring and at worst discriminatory, he can start to see why he has such ambivalence about taking up his own authority. He has a fear of becoming one of *them*.

This example highlights that this is inevitably an inexact project. There are a multitude of variables that impact what we do: personal history, past events, decisions, relationships and ecology all have some kind of impact. There are always too many things going on for us to ever exactly explain cause and effect. However, we can become aware of some of the contributors to our current dilemmas and what might influence our automatic or default reactions. Having this awareness can help us make progress.

Our experience of teaching and consulting with thousands of people exercising leadership in Australia has revealed distinct patterns of practice that impact the Australia sphere. We call these patterns the 'paradoxes of Australian leadership'. These paradoxes are clearly not exclusively Australian but they do strongly emerge *together* in the Australian context. They are not meant as a definitive and conclusive sociological analysis. Instead, we present them here because they strongly impact the practice of leadership in Australia. And because leadership in Australia is most often practised by Australians, we are frequently blind to the dynamics and unwittingly collude with them.

> *One fish looks at another and asks, 'So, how's the water?'*
> *The other fish replies, 'What's water?'*

We see these paradoxes play out in our daily work with managers, public servants, politicians, business owners and community leaders. They are:

1. Anti-authority and authority-dependent
2. Egalitarian and hierarchical

3. Relational and competitive
4. Battling adversity and living in prosperity.

These paradoxes give the globally held fantasy about leadership a specific Australian texture and complexity. Many Australians are relatively free to take up the role of leadership. This role is congruent with widely held social and community values and we are often motivated and encouraged to take up these roles. But we also have values, history and motivations that constrain us. These can be harder to identify or realise their impact. Just as fish take the water in which they swim for granted and are thus unaware of it, Australia is the water in which we swim.

The following chapters focus on raising awareness of the water we swim in before we look at practices for swimming more effectively.

CHAPTER 4

PARADOX 1

ANTI-AUTHORITY AND AUTHORITY-DEPENDENT

THE TENSION BETWEEN OUR DESIRE AND DEPENDENCY FOR AUTHORITY WHILE SIMULTANEOUSLY RAILING AGAINST IT

For we are young and free? The force of dependence

The First Fleet sailed into Port Jackson, Sydney, in 1788 in the same year as the American constitution was ratified. Those in charge of the arrivals had to quickly find a way to manage and provide for a dependent, diverse and homesick population. The first white settlers had little understanding of how to survive in the new landscape, and were dependent on a worryingly long and precarious supply line from the United Kingdom for survival. This first generation of white Australia, were dependent on their jailers for their survival. As a much younger and smaller set of disparate colonies, Australia was a long way from being ready to agitate for its independence from the UK as the Americans

had done in the preceding decade. (Although time would show that this was never a priority.) In contrast Australians held an enduring relationship with the mother country and focused on finding a way to make our disparate (white) population work in an adverse landscape while the British had our backs.

As the Americans finished their war of independence, Australia began a long and, in many ways, fruitful dependency. Over time that dependency has shifted from the mother country to local bureaucracy of government. Bureaucracy became the defacto imperial protector and director. It did this by creating systems and structures to provide for the colony and protect its inhabitants, constituting what writer Paul Kelly coined 'The Australian Settlement'.[1] It included, among other elements, wage arbitration, state paternalism and industry protection. All these structures

PARADOX 1: ANTI-AUTHORITY AND AUTHORITY-DEPENDENT

centralised equity and care for Australians and inevitably and perhaps unwittingly created a dependence on authority. This dependence dynamic went beyond white Australia.

As the white jailed population became the jailers of black Australia, they soon set about 'caring' for the Indigenous inhabitants. Many Indigenous (and non-Indigenous) Australians have since been advocating for their need to be free of the industry created around care-giving, that still positions them as dependent.

For all Australians the expectation of both protection and provision features more prominently than we may like to admit. For example, of the Americans who complain most bitterly about authority (government), many see the solution as having less government. In contrast, complaining Australians expect government to do more. Australian political commentator Laura Tingle hypothesised that our great expectations of government is something deeply embedded in the Australian culture:

> Since the deregulation era of the 1980s, governments can do less, but we wish they could do more. From Hawke to Gillard, each prime minister has grappled with this dilemma. Keating sought to change expectations, Howard to feed a culture of entitlement. Rudd to reconceive the federation. Through all of this, and back to our origins, runs an almost childlike sense of the government as saviour and provider that has remained constant even as the world has changed.[2]

We see this play out today in organisational and community life—we look to the centre or the top of our systems for help or to find someone to blame. It is interesting to note how often in Australian organisations approval is sought and deemed necessary from those further up the hierarchy—when so little of this approval is actually set out in position descriptions and organisational policy. There may be much talk of empowerment in Australian organisational life but it is a hard thing to propagate in the face of so much dependence, which we explain as a need to 'get approval'.

This is one way to explain our own and our leaders' reluctance to seek full independence for Australia. Repeated polls show that less than 50 per cent of Australians support a republic. Polling conducted by Morgan in 2011[3] showed support for the monarchy to be 55 per cent (up from 17 per cent in 1999, the same year of the failed national referendum on the issue of the republic). Support for a republic was at 34 per cent (down from 54 per cent in 1999). A 2008 poll that more thoroughly canvassed Australians' views on becoming a republic found that 31 per cent said Australia should never become a republic and 29 per cent said Australia should become a republic now. Most interestingly, 34 per cent said Australia should become a republic only after Queen Elizabeth II dies. Perhaps this is a natural transition point.

Some would say that we value being part of a network of international relationships in the Commonwealth and that a link to a previous time of tradition and ceremony is an important part of our history. A more cynical interpretation might be that we risk losing our pocket money if we annoy Mum. And what might that pocket money be? Certainty? Protection? Praise?

The comfort and lure of dependence

Whatever the reason, there is little momentum or energy in the public conversation about Australia becoming a republic. This is a long-term dynamic in Australian history. For example, in 1931, the British parliament legislated independence for self-governing dominions of the British Empire. Canada ratified the Act immediately and by 1934 so did South Africa. For Australia, the Act was largely symbolic as our independence from the United Kingdom was already a practical reality. Symbolism is important as symbols signify who we are, what we stand for and what we consider important. It was not until 1942, eleven years and four prime ministers later, that prime minister John Curtin adopted the Statute.

The motivation for its adoption was not independence as a republic. This was, as it is now, a no-win political issue. Instead, the motivation was recognition of the need for a new, and perhaps deeper, dependency. Australia was facing a significant military threat from Japan and had finally recognised that protection by British military forces was no longer certain. Curtin decided to clarify Australia's independence by ratifying the Act. This was more of an internal gesture towards Australians in recognition of our vulnerability than an external signal to the world concerning our independence. It cleared the way for and explained the development of a new dependency—an alliance with the United States.

Dependency and trust are not the same

So Australia switched from one protector to another. Did we start trusting this new protector? Perhaps for a brief while when we were under the most imminent threat of invasion from the north during the Second World War. Our parents' generation considered the US 7th fleet to be Australia's saviour. However, it wasn't long before the honeymoon with our new big brother was over and we returned to what we see now as a high level of dependence but low trust of authority. Australia was highly dependent, but did not pretend we liked it.

The relationship with the mother country was in many ways conflicted. We wanted the comfort of a protector but resented wanting the protection. This resentment is understandable given the superior role that Britain played with Australia in the early days—that of a jailer and supervisory colonial power. While Britain's formal power has dissipated in modern times, its cultural superiority remained intact until the mid-twentieth century. Australia was, after all, a subset of Britain both physically, culturally and psychologically.

This mixture of high dependence and low trust are not unique to Australia's geopolitical history. It is a dynamic that plays out in many areas of Australian life today. For example, when organisations shut down, relocate or retrench, we automatically expect those in authority to consult with us and protect us. Our role in the change is often as a bystander or victim. That is not to excuse those in power from their responsibilities and obligations but these expectations are difficult to live up to when our dependence is so high. As a result we often see authority turning up in the role of the tyrant or the benevolent father. Neither role is particularly effective to make progress.

Dependence on authority can also take more subtle forms. We have habitually depended on our imperial benefactor's scrutiny and judgement to make progress: big brother is watching us and evaluating. Even while resenting it, like we would a critical parent, we have needed at least some of this scrutiny for our growth and development. As author David Malouf observed, we have held a 'determination to do better than they had done. That is, our awareness of their scrutiny helped to keep us up to the mark'.[4]

If this is true it has clearly been important for our development and transition into an advanced and functioning first-world country. But it raises questions on how we view the role of authority. Is it as someone who sees the best in us and wants us to do well, or someone who sees the worst in us and is looking to criticise and judge? While we experience ourselves as 'one down' it is hard to break free of this simultaneous reliance and resentment.

It also begs the question of how we change this dynamic. Do we wait for those in authority to deem us worthy, or do we make that decision ourselves and change the relationship to power?

Relative power differences can make those with less power feel dependent, scrutinised and distrusted. In Australia, distrust characterises our relationship with authority and it permeates many aspects of our lives. This ranges from suspicion of the boss, to the distrust and antipathy we feel for our politicians. It's more than just a power differential, it's hailed as part of our national character. This brings up important questions:

- Where does this distrust of authority come from and how could it shift?
- What happens when we ourselves are the authority figure? Do we face the same distrust, dependence and resentment?
- Does this dynamic partly explain why Australians struggle to take up leadership roles?

The larrikin spirit

Most cultures are cynical about the use of power. What varies is how the cynicism displays itself and how intensely it is displayed. In Australia, cynicism is often open and manifests both culturally and structurally. Culturally it is positively described as the 'larrikin spirit'—mocking of authority and irreverent to rules and convention. The larrikin is an icon with particular resonance, perhaps because of Australians' general conservatism and obedience. In a very large jail the larrikin had a lot of room to move. If you live in a jail and are not the jailer, it's pretty cool to thumb your nose at those in charge. Taking on the jailers and later any other 'wowsers' and their increasingly limiting boundaries and rules was a significant source of informal power.

Many of the convicts were transported for crimes of political activism as agitators and union organisers. Before the end of transportation in 1840, more than 50 000 Irish 'rebels' had been exiled to Australia. Their mistrust of British authority was entrenched in decades of political and class oppression and warfare. It was transported along with their vehement independence as Catholics. The term 'larrikin' emerged from the shadow of convict history as a term of abuse. First coined around 1870, it was used to describe 'teenage, working class hell-raisers who populated dance halls and cheap theatres. Crucially, the early larrikins were female as well as male.'[5] To this day larrikins, past and present, are portrayed as likeable and respectable even when they originate from a criminal underclass. This glorification has a uniquely Australian flavour. Australian historian and social scientist Beverley Kingston asks:

> Why has larrikinism become accepted as a light-hearted excuse for all kinds of bad behaviour in Australia, whether from sportsmen, politicians or businessmen? No British prime minister or American president would be described approvingly as a hooligan or a hoodlum, but we have had several larrikin prime ministers.[6]

The larrikin is the cultural embodiment of our distrust and rebellion against authority. Combined with the emergence of the protection of labour and the rise of the union movement, the role of the larrikin also influenced the structures created to manage our distrust of authority.

PARADOX 1: ANTI-AUTHORITY AND AUTHORITY-DEPENDENT

In case we needed reminding of how important it is for us to be cautious of those in power, history provides an interesting set of bookends. In November 1907, the Australian Commonwealth Court of Conciliation and Arbitration delivered the Harvester Judgement. Despite this judgement being subsequently overturned by the High Court, it set the benchmark for and created the institution of a fair wage. This judgement was about power, not price. The president of the court, Henry B. Higgins, saw a strong need to work against the 'despotic power' of employers.

One hundred years later to the month, Kevin Rudd was elected as prime minister of Australia. The success of the Labor party campaign hinged on the promise to repeal the WorkChoices system introduced by the conservative Howard government in 2006. Workchoices was a particularly unpopular piece of legislation as it (among a number of other controversial changes) repealed unfair dismissal laws for smaller companies and limited legal strike action for unionists and collective representation.

The symbolism of these hundred-year 'bookends' in Australian history is significant. Both judgements, judicial and political, provide protection from those in power in how they treat and pay workers.

Australians begin with mistrust of authority. But why is this the case in such a prosperous nation? The 'good-hearted rebel' is a romantic idea but is not the whole story. It goes deeper than that. We have a history with authority that explains this mistrust.

Mistrust of authority

When we work with Australians on the role of authority, it is interesting how often the word 'authority' is misheard as 'authoritarian', a more negatively value-laden word. But this is no 'misunderstanding'. It signals our difficulties with the role of authority and manifests as a distrust of authority in ourselves and others. We take up and seek roles of authority, but struggle to genuinely occupy the role with intent, sincerity and humanity.

This is for good reason. On the whole, the shoes we fill don't smell so great. From the arrival of white settlers in Australia more than 200 years ago, authority has not done itself many favours. The behaviour of those with power and influence over the last few centuries has become the cultural and personal stories that Australians carry around with them every day. These authority stories have only emerged in the public domain in the last few years.

In 2007 prime minister Kevin Rudd apologised to the Stolen Generation for the forced removal of an estimated 100 000 Aboriginal and Torres Strait Islander children from their families. Removal of children was government policy from 1909 until 1969. It involved not only the government but also churches and welfare bodies. This was not the isolated act of one authority but a coordinated effort by a number of institutions, some of which purported to have 'ultimate authority' on their side. The practice was part of a broader government policy to breed out and assimilate Indigenous people and at that time was argued as being in their best interests. History has proved otherwise. Needless to say, discussion of authority and power in Indigenous communities has a heat and depth that can be overwhelming and heartbreaking.

These forced removals of Indigenous children provide a striking and tragic case-in-point of how the acts and motivations of authority can cascade through generations. The immeasurable suffering and loss will continue to be felt for many years. But it goes beyond effects to also causes and perpetrators. The nation which began through a process of 'forced removal' by authority

PARADOX 1: ANTI-AUTHORITY AND AUTHORITY-DEPENDENT

in the United Kingdom in turn forcibly removed Indigenous children from their families and Indigenous people from their own land. The jailed whites became the defacto jailers of black Australia. Abuse of power and authority lingers like a ghost and has repeated over time and culture.

This is just one example of forced removal among many. In 2009, the Australian government apologised to the 'Forgotten Australians': the 500 000 children who were removed from their families in the UK and placed in Australian institutions or foster care. These children were removed as part of a scheme that brought children from poor families in the UK to help populate Britain's former colonies. The scheme ran between 1920 and 1960 in not only Australia but also Canada and New Zealand. While some of the children were sent by their parents in the hope of a better life in Australia, others were forcibly removed under the Child Migrants Programme if they were already in state care. Some children were told their parents were dead. Many parents did not know their children had been transported to Australia.

The 2004 Forgotten Australians Senate Report found a 'litany of emotional, physical and sexual abuse, and often criminal physical and sexual assault'.[7] The scheme was characterised by widespread deprivation of food, education and health care for the children involved.

These abuses didn't just happen to immigrant children. Between the 1950s and 1970s many children and mothers fell victim to forced adoption policies. It is estimated that 150 000 unwed Australian mothers unwillingly had their babies taken by churches, welfare bodies and adoption agencies. The 2012 Senate Inquiry received hundreds of submissions that included accounts of coercion, trauma and ongoing mental health problems of the mothers involved.

A survey conducted in 2010 with 650 Forgotten Australians in Queensland found the proportion of those accessing government services appeared to be low. Despite the trauma of their past, many Forgotten Australians did not, or could not, make use of mental health services. Twelve per cent explicitly referred to a lack of trust in government or other authorities as a reason for not approaching these kinds of services. Some of the reasons given for not using general services included:

- 'For most of my life, I avoided them in fear of what they would do to me again.'
- 'I don't trust government people. I have been lied to by them all my life. I had to see a shrink when my husband died because I felt, and still do, that the . . . hospital killed him. Now I am back to being that lonely little girl who doesn't trust people any more . . .'
- 'I am afraid of the power they can have over me and I don't feel safe.'[8]

In total 100 000, 500 000 and 150 000 children were stolen, forgotten and forced. These are large numbers in a country of just over 22 million inhabitants. If we add to this the number of victims of child sexual abuse currently (one in five girls and one in nine boys), we can understand the issues we have in trusting authority. It's also understandable that we may be hesitant to take up that role ourselves. As we move through our communities and organisations, what stories about authority do we encounter or travel past—which do we carry with us? This failure of authority to fulfil its core role of providing protection, direction and order has been part of the Australian story for a long time.

Thankfully, the story can and is changing. National apologies accompanied by public recognition of these historic acts of abuse have been made by those in power over the last five years. This is beginning to rewrite the story about authority in Australia. It offers the opportunity for the practice of authority in Australia to include care, inclusion and compassion.

Implications of being mistrustful and dependent

Being both dependent yet mistrustful of authority is a challenging paradox for those seeking to use power responsibly. We face citizens and employees who are sceptical at best and at worst distrustful and fearful, while expecting to be looked after. We simultaneously want authority to protect and provide for us whilst we show our disdain for it. Our authority is both called for *and* deauthorised. We will often deauthorise ourselves before someone else does. When the role of authority has such a history, it's no wonder we struggle under its weight. We can become both dependent on the approval of those we are trying to lead while subconsciously colluding with a rebellion against the role.

As a result it is easy to confuse the role of leadership for being only a helper or, in political life, a community service. It is both of these things and more. The temptation to solely fill people's expectations is neither useful nor entirely possible. Dependent relationships are rarely positive, particularly not in the long term. Often the first destination for Australian's complaint *and* support in the face of adversity or difficulty is the offices of those in positions of authority. Yet many cultures around the world have little or no expectation that those in positions of authority and power will help them.

As Australia becomes more heterogeneous, with a broader mix of cultures, experiences and values, we are increasingly unlikely to expect or want the same things. It is impossible to please everyone.

It is no wonder that politicians in particular are trusted to be a community service and simultaneously despised. We can be very good at setting authority up to fail. Many authority figures set themselves up to fail by colluding in these expectations.

Pleasing most of the people for most of the time is important to maintain the role of authority. But it has its limitations. It doesn't help people solve their own problems or provide vision—in other words, to exercise leadership.

> Amanda is an executive in a federal government department in Canberra. She is responsible for addressing a growing and increasingly important systemic challenge for the department: one that is seriously impacting its clients and threatening its survival and reputation. The workforce and her colleagues at the same level are diverse but have one thing in common: they feel immobilised, tired and frustrated. As they begin to work together to address this challenge, they find they have something else in common. Like many other managers in Australia they have an antipathy to their senior executive team. They oscillate between anger at the senior team's inaction, to humour at their seeming incompetence. They can also see that the senior team is, like them, struggling to understand let alone tackle the challenge that the department faces. But whenever they begin to contemplate doing something different, it seems they need the approval and acknowledgement of the senior team. This is curious because they purport to not value or respect the views of their senior team. The dynamic of waiting for authority to act while being dismissive of authority is mirrored through every level of the department. The systemic challenges remain unaddressed.

Opportunities of the paradox

It may seem like there is little opportunity in this paradox to be effective, let alone be successful. There isn't a lot of room to move from this position, but there is some.

Firstly, there is an opportunity to rewrite the story of authority. A young nation with a troubling story of authority is still a young nation. While it can seem 'stuck', authority is not yet entrenched in thousands of years of history, expectation and failure. Nor is it too heavily institutionalised, or seen as a birthright. Every time people in authority act and use their power differently, it contributes to rewriting our story with authority.

Secondly, the expectation that authority should look after us can, at its core, be seen as positive. It is a helpful reminder that the purpose of authority and leadership is to be in service of others. The spirit of this service is a useful cultural value that can be used purposefully as long as it doesn't create dependency. This requires us to bring a level of consciousness and intention to how we take up and interact with the role of authority.

Finally, to see authority as a positive sum game rather than a negative one is crucial. The following excerpt from Judith Brett's book *Ordinary People's Politics* perhaps best sums up the opportunity and challenge in this paradox:

> When Mick was about twenty he joined the CMF [Citizen Military Forces]: 'I hated policemen, I hated teachers, hated anyone that tried to remove my authority, but I loved the army.' In the army discipline had a purpose, authority talked to you and explained its reasons, and it cared for you, taught you things you needed to know if you were to survive.[9]

Mick's seemingly inexplicable love of the army, which one could argue would remove much more of his authority, is at another level completely explicable and insightful. It is an invitation for everyone in authority to completely own his or her power. Rather than it being at the expense of others, it comes through authorising others to take up their responsibility and own their power—getting people in our organisations and communities to wake up and acknowledge their own formal and informal power and care for how they use it. This is a way out of dependence and a way into participation.

Accepting our power and using it well is easier said than done, but we believe this awareness and skill can be learned and developed. We explore this further in Chapter 10.

CHAPTER 5

PARADOX 2
EGALITARIAN AND HIERARCHICAL

WHEN THE VALUE WE PLACE ON EQUALITY IS IN TENSION WITH A NEED AND DESIRE FOR HIERARCHY

Australians came to believe that during the terrible eight months on Gallipoli, fixed features of the national character had been revealed. Australians were innocent and fit; stoical and laconic; irreverent in the face of hidebound authority; naturally egalitarian and disdainful of British class differences.

'THE WAR MYTH THAT MADE US', ROBERT MANNE, 2007[1]

An egalitarian dream

Australia prides itself on being an egalitarian state, a place where there is equality between citizens—politically, culturally and socially. This egalitarianism tends to manifest as equality of opportunity, rather than an expectation that we will all end up equal. The Department of Foreign Affairs and Trade describes us to the world in this way:

In most practical ways, Australia is an egalitarian society. This does not mean that everyone is the same or that everybody has equal wealth or property. But it does mean that there are no formal or entrenched class distinctions in Australian society, as there are in some other countries. It also means that with hard work and commitment, people without high-level connections or influential patrons can realise their ambitions.[2]

This is what we call the 'fair go', where we hold that everyone should have access to the same privileges. Our political and economic structures seek to provide these equal opportunities. Examples of their prevalence are arbitration commissions for wages, a strong history of unionism, social safety nets, our redistributive tax system and the desire for consensus in organisational and political life.

In leadership, Australian egalitarianism promotes freedom of expression; it provides protection from an overindulgence in power for power's sake and self-importance. As a broadly held social value, egalitarianism develops mechanisms to look after the whole and not just the fortunate. Most recognisably it underlines Australians' irreverence for power and authority, for which we are known and liked. In theory, it allows people to transgress hierarchical boundaries with the philosophy that everyone's voice is equal, worthy and counts. Egalitarianism is an important check and balance on power and plays to an important value in Australian life, that of social inclusion.

Yet where there is light there are often shadows. The shadow side of egalitarianism plays out as the 'tall-poppy syndrome', where Australians who have gained some form of merit or acclaim are criticised, attacked or resented for achievements which have elevated them above others. It seems to apply in declining order of intensity to politicians, business and government 'elites', academics, entertainers and (eventually) sportspeople.

Egalitarian societies

In egalitarian societies, men intent on commanding others are systematically thwarted in their attempts. The weapons used by their supposed inferiors are ridicule, manipulation of public opinion, and disobedience. The boastful hunter is cut down by jokes about his miserable catch, and the would-be chief who tries to order others around is openly told how amusing his pretensions are. The power of leaders is thus delineated by an alliance from below. Christopher Boehm, an American cultural anthropologist (who later took up research on chimpanzees), studied these levelling mechanisms. He found that leaders who become too proud or bossy, fail to redistribute foods and goods, or close their own deals with outsiders, quickly lose respect and support.[3]

Leading in Australia means that those in positions of authority are at risk of this 'alliance from below' to re-establish equality, at least in feeling. This alliance is more than a resistance to authority, as previously discussed. It also speaks to the egalitarian nature, of no-one seeming to get too far in front of or 'above' each other.

This desire to seem to be like everyone else, to be ordinary, can be felt strongly, particularly in very senior roles. Former prime minister John Howard described himself as an 'average Australian bloke', an extraordinary claim for a prime minister who was in effect the least average person in Australia. This downplaying of rank is not unique to Howard: he represented Australia's discomfort with power, while simultaneously dedicating his life to gaining and maintaining power to become anything but ordinary or average.

While the anti-authoritarian paradox is concerned with a rebellion against power and authority, this dynamic is more about membership, maintenance and the importance of the majority. As soon as the words 'above' and 'below' emerge, we are very quickly in the domain of class and rank. This is a much more uncomfortable area to discuss in Australia—surprisingly difficult given that Australia thinks of itself as a classless state. Perhaps this is exactly why it is difficult to discuss.

An easier place to begin is to talk about an alliance of the 'middle'—rather than below.

A preoccupation with the middle

> We don't have classes here as in England . . . I do not believe that the real life of this nation is to be found either in the great luxury hotels and the petty gossip of so-called fashionable suburbs

PARADOX 2: EGALITARIAN AND HIERARCHICAL

or in the officialdom of organised masses. It is to be found in the homes of people who are nameless and unadvertised and who ... see in their children their greatest contribution to the immortality of the race.

Robert Menzies's 1942 speech to 'The Forgotten People'[4]

It is not surprising that our longest serving prime minister could so well capture the Australian attitude to class. After all, national leaders need to speak to and understand their people's psyche. Menzies spoke to the romance of a new land, free of the suffocating class structures of its coloniser. Perhaps Menzies's words were also an unwitting advertisement. At the time of this speech Australia stood on the threshold of one of the largest waves of immigration in its history. The immigrants that would come to Australia in the ensuing 30 years were escapees and, in many instances, victims of class oppression in their own lands. With such a large proportion of these immigrants from the lower socio-economic classes, Australia represented an opportunity to begin again in a land perceived as having more equality and opportunity. It offered them a chance to move to the middle.

Menzies didn't mean that we don't have social classes in Australia. Rather, he was extolling the virtues of the middle class and promoting their protection. He was doing what many leaders who followed him would consciously do, speak to the middle class of Australia. Who else is the 'working family' to which the Gillard and Rudd Labor governments liked to refer, if not the middle class of Australia or aspirants to the middle? John Howard also spoke to the middle. Not only in how he framed himself but also in how he reached out to the 'Howard battlers'. This group were struggling to enter or remain in the middle class rather than battling to survive. It potentially also made the middle class feel good about themselves as it was a nice label to fit our egalitarian tradition.

We aim for the middle and are wary of the upper—or at least having the outward appearance of the upper. This may be why Australia is such an attractive place for visitors and has such a high standard of living by global standards. A desire to minimise class and economic differences is not only central to Australia's concept of itself but, if achieved, can and does have a real impact on living standards. A now famous and controversial study by Richard Wilkinson and Kate Pickett in 2009, called the 'Spirit Level',[5] found that inequality impacts health outcomes, literacy, crime levels and prevalence of mental health issues across all levels of society. The data the Spirit Level puts forward is that income equality benefits everyone and not just the poor.

A desire to be free of the class structures that exist in other parts of the world are not only what makes us Australian, but also what makes Australia a place in which we and others want to live. Unfortunately, as the Spirit Level study goes on to show, some of our desire for equality is more hope and rhetoric than reality. On a number of measures, we are not as equal as we would like to think.

A changing reality

Australia has more economic equality than the US or the UK. However, we do not compare well to many of the other developed countries. The Spirit Level found that compared to the largest 23 developed nations, Australia rates poorly in equality measures. It is only beaten in the inequality stakes by the UK, US, Singapore and Portugal. Our traditional self-image as the 'fair go' nation is no longer correct on income equality in international terms or

PARADOX 2: EGALITARIAN AND HIERARCHICAL

even compared to Australia itself 20–30 years ago. According to Richard Wilkinson, the nation has 'clearly had a very big increase in inequality . . . what is quite interesting is the mismatch between a national mythology of how you are as a nation and the facts'.[6]

Yet while we hold these egalitarian values in our hearts, we operate in a world that has changed. Australia and its government and organisations have grown, requiring more structure and hierarchy to manage what we have—not to mention our new global obligations and aspirations. We work in increasingly layered organisations and need to transact across multiple differences of formal and informal power. Exercising leadership can happen on any level, but if we operate in a system we can't avoid hierarchy. We are either engaging with those above us or occupying a senior role ourselves.

The emergence of larger hierarchies is not just a function of our economic growth and global pressures. Sol Encel, the late Australian sociologist, observed that this is a phenomenon that we have purposefully driven towards: 'Herein lies the paradox of egalitarianism in Australia: the search for equality of the redistributive kind breeds bureaucracy, bureaucracy breeds authority; and authority undermines the equality which bred it.'[7]

Perhaps not intentionally, our search for equality inevitably means we create more hierarchy to redistribute wealth to maintain and live up to our egalitarian values. Inevitably bureaucracy needs to get bigger to fulfil these services. Compared to our American cousins, the call for smaller government is rarely heard. This in itself is not a bad thing. As power increases there is always an inevitable requirement to increase governance so that power does not go unchecked.

Although we created the growth in hierarchy, it doesn't mean that we know how to deal with it. It can be uncomfortable to think of ourselves as operating in layers of hierarchy which are inherently unequal.

In a senior executive team of a large Australian organisation that we worked with, the team talked at length of the difficulty they experienced in getting the level below them to understand and take action on the strategic imperatives they had set. They saw this group below as too focused on their more local and functional agendas and not acting as representatives, communicators and facilitators for the broader organisational agenda and change initiatives. This is a difficult (and common) dilemma in any organisational setting and in any culture. It is by no means easy to fix. To the organisation's credit the conversation continued beyond the usual exasperated complaining.

The solution proposed by the group was 'just spending more time' with the level below in a non-formal setting (translation: non-hierarchical/more equal setting). That is, the pub. It was thought that this would bring the two levels closer together and break down some of the barriers between levels that were seen as the cause of the inaction.

In this typically Australian response, our preference for equality can hinder the progress of the harder work of transacting across rank and power. This work requires time and a focus on working much more clearly on purpose and role, the realities of making progress in a hierarchy. *Then* we can celebrate by going to the pub!

Who was more uncomfortable with the differences in rank in this situation? It is usually those with a higher position in the hierarchy who don't like to think of themselves as 'above', even while striving for promotion. In our experience those 'below' are not expecting those above to be equal in the hierarchy.

While Australians may resent or mistrust authority, they still want them to take up their role. They see the necessity for authority's functions. This plays out overtly in the family context. Adolescents do not want their parents to be their friends; they want them, albeit begrudgingly, to be their parents. Similarly, those 'below' are usually just waiting for the boss to 'just do what they're paid to do'.

The problem lies with us accepting our power when we are uncomfortable with culturally unpopular positions of rank.

Rank sensitivity

'Rank and title have no charms in the Antipodes', wrote an English gold-digger in the 1850s.[8]

The signs of inequality have always been there politically. Perhaps we have been blind to them. If these differences didn't exist they wouldn't provide such political traction. Who were 'Howard's battlers'? What group did the Rudd and Gillard governments call 'working families'? Are they a class? Why did the Howard government try to contrast and distance itself from the 'elite'?

Rank, which indicates the relative differences of power between us, is a charged topic in any cultural setting. In Australia the subject has a particular intensity because our espoused values about equality aren't always matched by the reality. The beneficiaries of equity and the 'fair go' in our organisations and communities are usually in the middle ground—the middle classes. From the middle it is harder and sometimes impossible to see how egalitarian values are *not* being lived for everyone. Particularly, those out on the edges of power, those with little or no power. We can see the mythology doesn't match reality when we look at gender and race equality. The hope for a completely egalitarian society is utopian, even if most Australians still espouse this hope.

The 'heat' surrounding rank pulls us back to the middle, a much more comfortable place to be. This preference is more than just accidental. For much of Australia's history, moving out of the middle was not economically or morally viable or even attractive. The economic advantages of getting ahead were too slight to be worth the trouble.[9] More importantly, to elevate oneself out of the middle might be seen as immoral, selfish or self-obsessed, a betrayal of family and class. That is perhaps what we fear and why we look to others who have done it and survived.

In many ways Australian egalitarianism manifests as an aspiration and orientation to a large middle ground. The middle can safely appreciate that they are not at 'the bottom' and purport to not want to be at the top. It may be comfortable to be in the middle, but exercising leadership, which requires understanding and working with differences of power and rank, is unfortunately rarely comfortable.

Implications of being safe in the middle

This tension between egalitarianism and hierarchy is a dilemma for leadership in Australia. On the one hand we hope for equality and are suspicious of individual progress and achievement, and on the other hand we want to rise above and progress.

While it is an undeniable antidote to hubris and tyranny, it also means that it is harder for Australians to own power and as a result take responsibility for the consequences of how we use that power. We stay safe in the middle where our egalitarian aspirations can remain unchallenged and unexamined. Inevitably, leadership becomes not only highly constrained but also divorced from the reality of the rank and power differences between us.

PARADOX 2: EGALITARIAN AND HIERARCHICAL

This has an inevitable downside. The rejection (at least ideologically) of our rank and power engenders an inevitable sameness, caution and mediocrity. This can look like we are committed to ordinariness.[10] It becomes safer for inspiration, individuality and uniqueness to come out in private life rather than in group life where leadership is required.

The competing forces of increasingly complex hierarchies and our egalitarian values lead to an inevitable sensitivity to rank. Rather than dealing with the difficulty of our inequity, we have two alternative responses:

- The neglect response—trying to seem equal and hence abdicating our role. Here we act like 'one of the ordinary gang'.
- The abuse response—throwing our weight around. Or what we unflatteringly call 'pulling rank'.

Both of these responses show our trepidation but also encourage us to accept and grow into our power. Like a new driver we are prone to oversteering. It shows us where we need to learn.

Opportunities of the paradox

> There are many things about the 1950s and 1960s that we would not want to keep—but one value worth trying to reclaim about that era was the sense of egalitarianism. Too much inequality strains the social fabric, threatening to cleave us one from another. Australia is a stronger nation when we act together than when we pull apart.
>
> Andrew Leigh, Federal Member for Fraser, 2012[11]

The opportunity for leadership is to leverage the usefulness and importance of our authority while protecting the values of egalitarianism. This requires us to capitalise on our egalitarian values in a more nuanced and positive way: one where acting together means pushing us all up as a collective rather than down. This is the purpose of exercising leadership—to find ways to work together for the benefit of the system as a whole.

Australia still has high social mobility and that means we have more leadership mobility than we realise—what we called 'room to move' in Chapter 1. In the increasingly complex and hierarchical nature of our work, denying our power and the differences between us will only get us so far. Both as individuals and as a nation we need to be willing to 'take a promotion' by accepting the power we have: a promotion that is not only beneficial for ourselves but for the entire system. The higher purpose of benefit for the whole system can provide the motivation and means to steer through this adaptation.

The way out is counterintuitive. It does not involve trying to make us more equal. The authors of *The Spirit Level* show the general impact of extreme inequality is to make people fear and mistrust one another more. Equality doesn't happen through bringing each other down. It is about bringing everyone up. The work of leadership means owning our rank and facilitating others to lead. This is not to be confused with the economic argument of a rising tide lifting all boats. History has shown that this 'invisible hand' does not lift all in the way we would hope. Its failure is that it is more hope than action. It won't happen on its own; it requires intention.

We are still learning the subtleties of steering. When we are able to work more subtly with power and rank, we are able to find a new middle path, one that runs between the polarities of either neglect or abuse of power. This is not a place where we can hide our power, but one where we can hold both the value of equality and the potential of power. When we can accept our power and use that to define more purposeful roles, we can use it for the benefit of our organisations and communities.

CHAPTER 6

PARADOX 3

RELATIONAL AND COMPETITIVE

AUSTRALIANS' STRONG DESIRE FOR POSITIVE SOCIAL RELATIONSHIPS CREATES TENSION WITH A DESIRE TO INNOVATE AND COMPETE

Australian work life is traditionally and inherently relational. We enjoy a culture of 'mates' and 'mateship' and value relationships and informal settings in which friendships occur and develop. The Australian work context is unique in this way compared to other countries. Although mateship has an inherently male connotation and application, it is part of a broader Australian dynamic of informality, regardless of gender. Previous prime minister John Howard described this as 'comfortable and relaxed'. Those of us who entered their careers in the 'she'll be right' days may remember with humour (and some nostalgia) there being no expectation to return from the pub after Friday lunch. If you did, you returned to an office with no computers, a desk phone without voicemail and at worst a few faxes or telexes which could wait til Monday . . . or maybe Tuesday.

PARADOX 3: RELATIONAL AND COMPETITIVE

A global economy, internet, email and mobile communication ended these indulgences. Those days may now be gone forever, but there is still a search for comfort in the relationships of the Australian workplace. Australians are now working longer and harder, but the informality found in many of our workplaces has not changed. This can be seen in the inherent casualness in relations between different levels of power—particularly compared to our Asian neighbours. It is unusual to hear a superior addressed by 'Mr' or 'Ms' outside of a school classroom in Australia. Australian ideals of mateship are a good fit with our value of egalitarianism. What better way to seem equal than for all of us to be mates?

John Howard recognised this link to our values and sought to have 'mateship' introduced into the preamble of the Constitution at a referendum in 1999. Australian poet Les Murray drafted the proposed change: 'Australians are free to be proud of their country and heritage, free to realise themselves as individuals, and free to pursue their hopes and ideals. We value excellence as well as fairness, independence as dearly as mateship.'[1]

While Howard felt that mateship held 'a hallowed place in the Australian lexicon', he eventually dropped the proposal after clear signals from the Australian Democrats that the changes would not pass in the Senate. Murray for his part was also not supportive of the inclusion believing, among a number of reasons, that it was too 'bloke-ish'. It didn't make the constitution, but mateship eventually found its way into the Australian citizenship test. This hints that mateship may be just as much about exclusion as it is about inclusion. It raises the question of whether our preference for relationships is about seeking ways to include or exclude people. Who is 'in' and who is 'out'?

Mateship in our DNA?

> The Great Lone Land of magnificent distances and bright heat; the land of Self-reliance, and Never-give-in, and Help-your mate.[2]

There are good historical reasons for this preference for relationship. Facing a hostile environment and a superior and distant mother country, the colonial-convict settlement of early Australia relied on good relations for survival. But it was more than just survival. For Australian poet Henry Lawson, mateship was undeniably a mark of personal nobility, ironically most often displayed by the marginalised underclass of Australian society.[3]

These early norms established the relational culture we see today where being one of the mates is important. It gives us informal authority and builds trust and safety. It is another thread in the tapestry of Australians' irreverence for authority. Mates can

PARADOX 3: RELATIONAL AND COMPETITIVE

form an 'alliance from below' against those with power and keep each other safe. It is a clear manifestation of our egalitarian values.

If mateship was purely a function of adversity and a source of power against the more powerful, it would have probably disappeared as Australia became more prosperous. Instead we see the modern-day equivalent—'the boys' club'—is very much alive and powerful. This manifestation of our relational culture is an often invisible network of influence, advice and favour being played out in the upper circles of Australian life.

The dynamics of mateship are much deeper in our DNA than we may realise, having withstood the tests of time and changing circumstances. It is perhaps one of the strongest themes in our Anzac Day celebrations. Anzac soldiers are honoured for working together to support each other in the face of insurmountable challenges at the behest of a careless, hierarchical and distant imperial power. Indeed, mateship is advertised as one of the 'soldierly qualities' that the Australian Army seeks to instil in its recruits.

The function of mateship provides a convenient middle path between friendship and collegiality. We can retain the security of inclusion and fraternity without the downside of too much responsibility. It has been argued that this kind of relationship and the ideal within it has become a defacto patriotism. Patriotism tends to be regarded with some cynicism by Australians. In anything but the sporting domain it is viewed with caution. More so given the use of the Australian flag and Southern Cross in the infamous race riots at Cronulla Beach in Sydney in 2005. In contrast, loyalty and commitment to each other as mates has a powerful emotional appeal.[4] So while we may be sceptical of too much loyalty to country, this caution does not extend to scepticism of a loyalty to one's mates.

Organisational leaders often face the same caution when trying to rally loyalty to the organisation in times of change or hardship.

Change is usually trumped by the maintenance of positive and stable social relationships. Yet, exercising leadership often means surfacing the different and often competing loyalties and values. This can represent a threat to the existing cohesive relationships where not putting these loyalties first may be felt as a betrayal. Disloyalty to relationship is treated harshly in any culture, not just Australia. But the primacy of relationships emerges so strongly in organisational life in Australia that a disloyalty to relationship can often get treated in the same way as assertion of higher power and rank. You might get accused of being 'up yourself'.

> One Australian retailer began as a collection of young entrepreneurs. With humble beginnings from the back of a truck and borrowed garages, the business soon grew to many stores and a complex web of supply chains. One of the most difficult aspects of the growth was shifting from a culture where the two 'mates' were at the centre of all decisions and thinking, to one where the group could become a professionally run organisation with delegated responsibilities and clear roles and accountabilities. This was no easy task. Learning how to deal with competing commitments, loyalties, ambitions and priorities meant challenging the preferred dynamic of working through relationships alone.

It is dangerous to be too critical of the mates dynamic. In many ways it plays an important role, particularly in certain contexts of adversity when the situation is uncertain or unpredictable or when innovation and a fast response is required. Good relationships are essential to the survival of any system and can be a very effective shortcut to make progress. Relationships can work as a defacto for hierarchies, clear roles and established processes. Trust becomes

PARADOX 3: RELATIONAL AND COMPETITIVE

the basis of the work instead. However, trust requires that we share similar values, culture and assumptions which build the common ground to work together. Combined with competence, this platform can be formidable, particularly in the early stages of development for smaller organisations.

While mateship's male focus has been called into question, there has been little questioning of the more endemic focus on relationship in daily organisational and community life. It is generally assumed that strong relationships are desirable and something we should seek to build. They are important but, unfortunately, they are not enough.

Taking up a leadership role now requires us to tackle diverse, complex challenges with a range of stakeholders who often have competing needs and agendas. In this context, a reliance on relationships becomes less effective and usually only serves the 'in group'. Organisations often face this dilemma when they move past the start-up stage and are developing into a large functioning system. Similarly, this challenges managers who are transitioning from single functional roles to having broader, cross-functional responsibilities across the whole system. The reliance on relationship typically benefits only some members of the system. It relies on a stable system in which the players and the context don't change. Not only is this unsustainable, it limits the development of the necessary processes, systems and infrastructure without a reliance on key people in the inner circle.

Works for me(n)

Richard joined a large Australian organisation in a two-stage interview process. Perhaps interview is too generous a description. While he hadn't applied for a role in the organisation, a 'mate' recommended he speak to the CEO. Richard and the CEO hit it off and he was invited to think about joining the organisation. When he asked about the role, the response was that it would be created around the skill-set that he brought. But first he had to meet the chairman. In this meeting, Richard and the chairman had oblique discussions on life in general. Richard felt that his faith was being tested. It was a surprise to Richard and the rest of the organisation when he was offered a role. He felt that his competence for the role wasn't tested or questioned. He had been 'blessed' and was seen as a good bloke.

Mateship is still predominantly masculine, serving the traditional holders of power in Australia. Women have been traditionally excluded from the boys' club. Moreover, the military associations support and reinforce their power and resonance for men and by men. This club relies on strong relationships often forged and maintained in informal contexts such as pubs, sports clubs or games usually only attended by the boys. This extends into our boardrooms and echelons of senior management where women are often still on the outside looking in.

But it would be a mistake to assume that mateship applies only to men. While it definitely has benefited men much more than women, and is still picked up much more by men, the relational tone of the club crosses gender boundaries and appears in some form in most Australian contexts. Women who pick up the role of generating and maintaining relationships also see the benefit of mateship to make progress: the focus on maintaining relationships without a clear transactional motivation often build solid relationships that can be leveraged when needed. This works partly for some women but they are often still beholden to a male mateship network to get ahead.

PARADOX 3: RELATIONAL AND COMPETITIVE

Mateship has a purpose. Systems cannot function without working relationships. However, when it is the dominant dynamic, it stops serving the purpose of a system at some point. This is usually when the relationships start getting in the way of the organisational challenges or when those who are not one of the mates become excluded. This exclusion is the inevitable downside of a culture dominated by relationships. Unfortunately, it is often difficult to see who and what is excluded as well as the impact of the exclusion on those outside the inner circle. If you are inside the circle—where authority almost always sits—it is usually most difficult to see.

At mateship's most benign there are those who are left out of the loop. They strive to sit at or get to the table. At its worst mateship can marginalise those who are not part of the circle. In Australia this has been most keenly felt by women in, or aspiring to be in, leadership roles. As Larissa Behrendt, Professor of Law and Director of Research at the Jumbunna Indigenous House of Learning at the University of Technology, Sydney, reflected:

> We have to be honest about the fact that all we've achieved is getting more women into positions of power. We haven't done anything to change the power structure or to change the priorities of home and family and work. A lot of women play the game a certain way and they're really good at it. But there's no solidarity about changing it so it's easier for other women. The women that survive in those professions [law] are the ones who can play the game.

When the 'mates' set the rules and culture, it often only works for the inner circle. As Larissa's example above shows, those in the outer circle can end up being 'colonised' with the accepted values and behaviours. For example, working mothers may find that all the important meetings happen at a time that suits only some employees. One senior executive from the public service faced inexplicable resistance from her colleagues to shift a weekly 7.45 a.m. meeting, when she had to drop off children, to later in the day. The response was, 'This is just when *we* have these meetings' (our italics). Another female executive from a large Australian corporation lamented that she realised it was impossible for her to do that role at the same intensity as her male peers without her 'own wife' to organise her home life.

It is inevitable that currently men are the beneficiaries and advocates of the relational preference, having traditionally held the roles of power in Australia.

The need for relationship remains as a primal yearning but mateship is not enough in this new world. Something else has emerged which is more difficult for us to name and deal with productively. This is another essential part of us—our competitive side.

The shadow side of mateship: competition

Australians are comfortable when competing with each other and anyone else in the sporting domain. We have a perverse expectation that we punch above our weight and win against larger and better-financed nations. In sport, we seem to have found a way to reconcile our relational culture with this competitive drive. The overwhelmingly popular, annual rugby league showdown between the states of New South Wales and Queensland (the State of Origin) is a dramatic demonstration of our desire to compete. Indeed, it has been advertised in characteristic hyperbole as 'State vs. State: Mate vs. Mate'.

However, outside of the sporting domain our competitive nature is harder to reconcile with our preference for relationship.

The inevitable competition for power between individuals in society and organisational life is difficult to discuss. The rise of consumerism and individualism in Australian life shows the increasing value we place on the rights and freedoms of the individual in economic and social life: what might be called 'small l' liberal values.

This tension between the values of the individual and the collective plays out in the channelling of wealthier or academically smarter children away from public schools as a result of significant increases in federal funding for private schools. Public schools are substantially less well resourced. This approach is unique to Australia when compared to funding arrangements for education in other OECD (Organisation for Economic Co-operation and Development) countries.

On the one hand, we want our children to have the best possible opportunities for success in the future. Parents who have the means try to achieve this by sending their children to private and selective schools. They want their children to be able to compete with others entering the workforce. On the other hand, parents also see schools as important social building blocks: places where children can learn to interact across difference in culture and socio-economic background.

The impact is the draining of public schools. Children who are less academically gifted or from less privileged families are being left behind and our school system is becoming stratified by social class, despite our strong desire for equality of opportunity. Our inability to reconcile these two values can be found in the 'spirited' debate or 'no-go' discussion areas between parents. As a result politicians face increasing difficulty in delivering comprehensive reforms to education and educational funding in Australia.

We have difficulty reconciling the competing values of egalitarianism, mateship and individualism in this long-standing education debate—hence the paradox. Admitting to this individualism and competition and the challenge that they present to our values is difficult.

This incongruence appears in organisational life, too. Competition for resources, attention or power between departments or individuals rarely takes place formally. Instead there is a rhetoric of equality that denies the inevitable disparities of power and resources. In numerous organisations where we have worked, there is a high level of 'civility' in executive team meetings which gives the appearance of good relationships. But the capacity of these teams to have open discussion or process disruptive or individual agendas is often limited. This doesn't mean that the competition doesn't happen—it just happens behind closed doors. As a result, innovation becomes difficult because it can be interpreted as a form of competition for existing relationships and power.

Similarly, individual ambitions don't go away just because they are not talked about. Perhaps if we were more open about our ambitions, both systemically and individually, there could be discussion on how to support them in a way that is of benefit to our organisations (not just for those in the inner circle). We might see that there are people in our organisations who want the top jobs and we can support them in their development to reach them.

Implications of mateship and competition

Our lack of skill in interacting with others through our formal roles inevitably puts relationship ahead of purpose. This means that it can be dangerous or counter-cultural to put organisational purpose ahead of relationship. We go from being mates to the role of authoritarian boss with seemingly little space for anything in between.

As well as marginalising others, the culture of mateship can lead to a lack of innovation and stifle the creativity that comes from conflict and diversity. We walk familiar ground rather than necessary ground, not to mention the costs of hiring and doing business with those we like rather than those most competent for the role and purpose.

> If you look across the whole Australian market, people are blind to talent that doesn't look like them. It's conscious and unconscious bias, and people are lazy. No-one's had to worry about it much before because everything's been fine.
>
> Ann Sherry, CEO, Carnival Australia

Relationships are important and will develop and deepen, but leadership requires us to think of the whole and not just look after those we have good relationships with or avoid things that may jeopardise them. Working with different values and groups is another way of talking about the skill of working politically. This is a difficult skill to admit to needing for many Australian managers. We have problems owning the political dimensions of our role and instead tend to project all our anxiety about politics onto politicians. Perhaps this is why politicians are so reviled in Australia. We project onto them what we are uncomfortable owning ourselves, particularly our competitive side.

Ironically, denying competition and ambition inevitably promotes the aspects of working politically which are the most reviled. We end up with backroom deals carried out in the shadows and discussions which favour some and not others.

Finally, and perhaps most importantly, the increasingly heterogeneous nature of Australian working and political life will promote in- and out-groups if we continue to do business the way we do now. Prioritising relationships over purpose means that those with less or more rank often get left out. Invariably they are the very people who bring a useful perspective to the challenges we face.

Opportunities of the paradox

Is it acceptable to be competitive anywhere but in sport and politics in Australia? When we deny our ambitions, it is hard to use our energy, creativity or the potential of our individualism to positively impact others.

The opportunity in Australia is to use our informality and warmth in relationship in concert with a much clearer and stronger ownership of the roles of leadership. This is covered in depth in Chapter 11, where we explore a concept of role which is broader and more purposeful than the traditional idea. It is the role of leadership which enables the whole system to make progress, not just for your faction and friends. We may become mates that can mobilise attention to an issue and deal with problems by using our difference. We can also seek to improve mobility between different levels of hierarchies so that power is dispersed. To do this requires us to accept our rank and the role of authority.

Australia has an opportunity that few other countries have in the context of leadership. People in positions of authority can use their formal roles and personal relationships to model a type of leadership that is both caring and responsible for the whole. This kind of power is what the world needs more of, and where Australia could lead. We are unencumbered by the more established boundaries of class and position that Europe carries. This give us the opportunity to lead by leveraging the differences and similarities that exist in culture and class. It means being able to express the confidence that comes from our similarities and trust the expression of our differences. If we can build our capacity to facilitate difference and conflict, particularly among mates, we can harness the innovation that will likely arise.

CHAPTER 7

PARADOX 4

BATTLING ADVERSITY AND LIVING IN PROSPERITY

CARRYING A STORY OF ADVERSITY AND RELYING ON CRISIS TO LEAD WHILE AT THE SAME TIME ENJOYING A HIGH LEVEL OF PROSPERITY AS A COUNTRY

Australia as 'battlers'?

Bushfires, floods and cyclones reawaken the increasingly urban population to the reality of the Australian environment. We don't have to go out bush or wait for the arrival of a natural disaster to reconnect with adversity: it sits deeply in our DNA. Indigenous Australia had been adapting to environmental adversity for thousands of years before they were faced with adversity of a different kind—the dispossession of their land. Early European settlers faced a seemingly hostile and mysterious landscape with little help or skill. They also felt 'threatened' by an Indigenous population they didn't seek to understand or partner with, creating even more hardship and difficulties for themselves.

PARADOX 4: BATTLING ADVERSITY AND LIVING IN PROSPERITY

Adversity brought early settlers together in the same way it does now when we face natural disasters. The community spirit and cooperation following the Victorian bushfires in 2009 and the Queensland floods in 2010 showed not just how Australians can pull together, but also highlighted the important part adversity plays in our national story.

We don't have a lower class, we have 'battlers' who are 'doing it tough'. These are marks of pride in contrast to what might be seen as a negative class marker in another society.

In our work with change agents from across all sectors, it is striking how often the topic of crisis emerges in discussions about leadership. Australians find it easier to conceive or take up an authority role in the context of a flood, hurricane or other emergency. Crisis may provide an authorisation that evades us normally; perhaps the adrenalin of crisis supersedes a normal fear of stepping up and owning our authority or disrupting the 'relational' status quo. This raises some important questions. How do we lead without hardship? Do we need to create a crisis to feel authorised? These are also global questions and not limited to Australia. More specific to Australia is the question of can we lead in prosperity and how do we do that? Leadership is more difficult when we are not doing it tough.

In the absence of adversity, are we willing to pick up the responsibilities that come with prosperity and privilege?

Prosperity? Australia?

The last twenty years have seen unprecedented economic prosperity in Australia. It wasn't always so. In 2006, departing Reserve Bank governor Ian Macfarlane spoke of Australia's emergence from its recession in 1991: 'A brooding pessimism seemed to affect all shades of economic and political opinion and little hope was held for our economic future.'[1]

At the time unemployment sat at 11 per cent. In Sydney the opening of a new family restaurant chain made the news as more than 200 people queued around the corner to get an interview for a handful of award-wage jobs. Things have certainly changed.

Today, there are few nations that can match Australia's economic growth and prosperity. In the 1990s Australia ranked in the bottom third for GDP (gross domestic product) growth per person. In 2012 Australia is in the top third (5th).[2] And it's not just about the money. According to the United Nations, Australia ranked second in the Human Development Index in 2011; and in 2012 was ranked in *The Economist*'s Intelligence Unit where-to-be-born index as the 'second-best country in the world to be born', just 0.1 points behind Switzerland.[3] It would appear that on a range of indicators Australia is indeed 'the lucky country'.

PARADOX 4: BATTLING ADVERSITY AND LIVING IN PROSPERITY

A good share of the working population has never experienced an economic recession and a number of generations have become accustomed to unprecedented material comfort and success. Few of us today have ever experienced real hardship. When we put the idea that Australia has been in an economic boom for a long time to our colleagues, all those under 35 said, 'What boom?' This lack of appreciation of Australia's relative prosperity was echoed by a Boston Consulting Group survey in 2012 that found consumer sentiment is as low in Australia as it is for some of the European nations suffering the worst of the debt crisis.[4]

Australia has routinely rated globally as one of the top three countries in the world in terms of standard of living. Clearly, not everyone is sailing yachts around Sydney Harbour and income inequality is getting wider, but it's hard to argue with Australia's relative prosperity from a global perspective.

How does this prosperity fit with our story of adversity? It doesn't. We see this at a national political level in the difficulty of thinking beyond the present or beyond our immediate shores. In the mid-1980s, *The Economist* magazine summed up Australia in the following terms: 'If you look at history, Australia is one of the best managers of adversity the world has seen—and the worst manager of prosperity.'[5]

How we define prosperity highlights the paradox we sit in. As outlined in Chapter 5 Australia's GDP growth has also brought with it growing inequity and disparity between the 'haves' and the 'have nots'. As Simon Sheikh, former director of GetUp, an independent community advocacy organisation, observed: 'It's not about our national output, it's about how equally that national output is spread which determines whether we are a country that's leading.'

This reflects the challenge of this paradox and asks us to think about who we are as leaders in prosperity. Are we able to acknowledge our prosperity when increasing numbers of people are living in poverty, or can we only lead well in crisis?

Addicted to crisis and complaining, or just complacent?

> [There] can be only one answer: we are, as a nation, chucking a full-on, all-screaming, all-door-slamming teenage temper tantrum.[6]

Are we spoilt adolescents? Or just frustrated and struggling to deal with our power and privilege? This frustration and pessimism has a deeper impact on how we see our world than is reflected in our confidence as consumers. Recent research suggests that there is a gap between how we perceive ourselves and the reality of how we are faring as a country. A national values assessment by the Barrett Values Centre in 2009[7] was conducted to determine the values of Australians and their perception of how those values were lived. 'Entropy' is a term used by the centre to show the gap between the positive values expressed and those that are perceived as dysfunctional. Their research found that Australia's level of entropy was at 42 per cent.

> To put this in perspective, when we see organisations with anything above 10 [per cent] entropy, we say they need to quickly address issues to avoid serious financial repercussions. [Australia's] 42 per cent indicates the potential for collapse, both socially and financially. When we look at the words that are associated with entropy we see these themes:
>
> - Lack of confidence in the ability of leaders to make decisions based on integrity
> - Lack of accountability and lack of ability to be good stewards of resources

PARADOX 4: BATTLING ADVERSITY AND LIVING IN PROSPERITY

- Focus on material gain while people lack opportunity and necessities
- Culture that allows hostility to breed.

Most of the values for the Current Culture are what we call potentially limiting. This indicates a high level of frustration, cynicism and fear about the state of the Current Culture.

The Barrett Centre goes on to draw a link between high levels of entropy and the systemic collapse of a number of nations. For example, Argentina (prior to the 2001 financial crisis) had 60 per cent entropy, and the USA (prior to the global financial crisis in 2007/2008) had 52 per cent entropy. These nations had serious structural problems that could explain some of this entropy and subsequent failure. But how do we explain 42 per cent in Australia, with a solid economic foundation and functioning institutions and systems? In the Barrett Centre's view, this level of entropy 'indicates leadership issues that if left unaddressed could lead to significant social unrest'.[8]

This level of dissatisfaction with leadership reflects the challenge of this paradox. The lure of seeing ourselves as battlers may spur us to keep striving for improvement, but it also raises questions not only of who we trust to lead us but *when* we will trust. Will we allow ourselves to lead and be led only in adversity and in emergencies? We see how addicted to emergency leaders are on the political stage. The future takes a back seat to the smaller and local problems, 'crises' and scandals of the present.

This short-term crisis orientation creates a leadership culture of response rather than of vision and purpose. We work with senior leaders in all sectors and see how difficult it is to move out of a 'response mode' generated by the latest issue or problem. It is rare to hear discussions of the future. Discussing purpose is often difficult and irritating. Instead, time is usually consumed feeding the 'urgent' needs of a response via our smartphones: an ever-ready distraction from the harder work of focusing on the future and a higher purpose.

Perhaps this is all we want from leadership. In positions of authority we are always representing other Australians' values and needs; it can be difficult for us to do otherwise. In the *What Matters to Australians Report* of 2012 by the Anatomy of Civil Societies Research Project its authors found:

> What is perhaps most obvious is that local issues dominate global issues... the results reveal that the most salient issues for Australians in the conduct of their lives are those most immediate and closest to their personal welfare. Food and health, local crime and safety, and rights to basic services are their top three concerns. Australians are effectively indifferent to global and societal issues, rating these significantly lower.[9]

We are a product of our culture and in positions of authority we need to be responsive to our culture's demands. Roles of authority may come more easily to those adept at handling problems and adversity than to those who can look to the longer term or the advancement of a larger system. This presents a challenge if we want to exercise leadership in Australia and try to mobilise people's attention on the harder, longer term challenges we face.

Implications of adversity and prosperity

A lot can be learnt about the limitations of an adversity mindset from the literature on crisis management. Crisis, like adversity, presents us with threat and uncertainty. This is a natural and comparatively safe environment in which to be authorised to 'just do something'. Moreover, there is a popular myth that difficulties and crises create a 'burning platform' for reform of institutional structures and long-standing policies.[10] This opportunity is often overrated.

The requirements of crisis are often quite different to what is required for longer term reform. Orientating systems and people to the future and changing cultures is a different type of work than responding to the present difficulties. While adversity, like crisis, can bring us together to face a common problem, it can also keep us stuck in the short term and the present. It often focuses us on a response which quickly returns us to the status quo rather than helping us address some of the fundamental issues which may have caused the crisis in the first place.

Similarly, thinking we face constant adversity keeps us concerned with making things easier and avoiding the harder adaptive work. This dynamic has been particularly strong in the political context in recent years. Australia's ongoing challenge as more refugees seek asylum demonstrates this bind. More and more boats continue to arrive on Australia's shores and many asylum-seekers have died in their endeavour to get here. Successive governments have been under increasing pressure to act, trying many short-term technical solutions. This does little to help us think of the future because we are stuck in maintaining or restoring the comfort of the present.

This is the rub. Without difficulty and adversity, all we want from our leaders is to do what is required for us to remain comfortable. We can never be comfortable enough and don't like it when that comfort is threatened. An adversity mindset instils dependency on leadership to comfort us. Not an inspiring job description for leadership or for us.

Finally, and perhaps most importantly, constantly thinking we have it tough means we are participating in a denial of our privileges and power. We are at risk of squandering our gifts. It means that all we have to do with our privilege is to show it and not to use it. This not only keeps us comfortable but encourages mediocrity and colludes in our complacency.

Opportunity of the paradox

Authority's role in prosperity is to exercise leadership: to go beyond maintenance and challenge the norms of the status quo. Instead of continuing the cycle of complaint and dependency, we need to do something counterintuitive to our self-deprecating nature. Can we be more generous with ourselves? Generous enough to see that we have something to offer the world, our workplaces and communities?

Admitting to our privilege is hard. It doesn't fit with the story Australians have of being battlers or the underdog. Owning our privilege may allow us to instil vision in Australian leadership, something which is sorely missed. To create a vision we need to look up and beyond ourselves.

Firstly, we can start to talk about the vision that we have for ourselves as Australians. Who do we want to be in the world and do we want to demonstrate what it means to use privilege well? If we aspire to use our privilege, we need to think about being a global player with intentionality rather than a spectator. This applies at the local and organisational level as well. There is an opportunity to exercise leadership that lifts organisations, sectors and communities rather than maintaining the same-old-same-old. We have an opportunity to snap out of the mediocrity that we think is required. We can be generous and ambitious.

Secondly, we can start to demand that our leaders begin to look upwards and outwards. We need to authorise them and ourselves to be ambitious, visionary and bold. We have evidence that we can do this. Our current prosperity did not come about overnight. It is the product of reforms undertaken in the 1980s that saw Australia move away from protectionism to being one of the most open economies in the world. The Productivity Commission, the Australian government research and advisory body on economic, social and environmental issues, found that these policy reforms were a major factor in Australia's recent growth.

> Social Leadership Australia (SLA) has been working with the National Australia Bank for more than five years. The bank has invested heavily in developing the social leadership capacity of its senior managers. A key part of this process involves senior executives spending time in communities such as remote Indigenous communities, prisons and refugee organisations. The bank sees this process of 'waking up' their executives as crucial for them to lead well within the bank system. They contend that to do that they need to understand and consider their role in the broader world. By having more awareness of what is happening within the communities the bank operates in, they can start to make decisions in the best interests of the community as a whole—as well as for the bank. For the bank executives, this process of waking up to and owning rank and privilege is uncomfortable and challenging. Yet it is improving not only how they use their power internally, but is also changing the conversations and internal narrative about what they do with that power outside of their four walls.

We are at an important point in our history of developing prosperity. It is unlikely to come again in our lifetimes. There is an opportunity and need for us to lead in a way that recognises the advantage of our position.

> Australians must now decide what sort of country they want their children to live in. They can enjoy their prosperity, squander what they do not consume and wait to see what the future brings; or they can actively set about creating the sort of society that other nations envy and want to emulate.
>
> *The Economist,* May 2011[11]

To 'triumph over adversity' is a well-used phrase to tell the story of individuals who have succeeded against the odds. The opportunity is there for our grandchildren in 40 years time to say that we were able to 'triumph with prosperity'.

That will require a change in how we lead: adversity requires doing—prosperity requires thought.

PART 3
SHIFTING PRACTICE

CHAPTER 8

LEADING ACROSS DIFFERENCE— THE GREAT AUSTRALIAN CHALLENGE

The following section presents a number of capabilities that can, in our experience, transform the way we think about and practise leadership in Australia. The preceding two sections looked at what is going on in Australia from a leadership perspective and offered some hypotheses about why these things might be happening. The paradoxes of leadership in Australia are a way to think about what might get in the way of leading better and also the opportunities inherent in the paradoxes. Unsurprisingly they mostly revolve around how we perceive, relate to and use our power and authority.

Core to making progress on the paradoxes of leadership is how we use our authority to address one of the biggest challenges and greatest opportunities for change—what we call *leading across difference*. These are differences of competing values, preferences, needs and interests. They are part of every leadership challenge that we are likely to encounter. Working across difference exposes many of the paradoxes of leadership in Australia discussed earlier, when inevitably we have to deal with issues of authority, competition, equality and the type of relationships we have with each other. When we are:

> ... struggling to tackle more intricate problems whose causes and consequences pay no attention to the boundaries we have created ... Issues spill over more quickly into adjoining agencies and neighboring jurisdictions. As the world becomes flatter, many local issues reach around the world and many global issues have local implications.[1]

Our world is rapidly changing. Every day we become more reliant on those around us for our continuing stability and prosperity. The world's problems are our problems: climate change, energy management, asylum-seekers and religious extremism to name a few. Australia itself is also becoming increasingly diverse. In the 2012 census, Australia's biggest city, Sydney, had more than one-third of its citizens born overseas. Our ability to do business solely with 'people like us' is quickly diminishing. Diversity is now becoming the mainstream. While that brings opportunity and creativity, it inevitably also brings more conflict.

Increasingly we are being called upon to be innovative. We can't do this work alone—neither as Australia the nation or as Australians. Nor can we do it alone within our own sector, function, value set or culture. We cannot rely on authority to have the answers to these challenges. The solution to many of our toughest challenges lies in their co-creation with others.

These times call for leadership across a diversity of difference. Geoff Gallop, former premier of Western Australia, argues this kind of leadership means:

> ... accepting complexity. We're in a much tougher period since September 11. The type of leadership required now is quite different. Leadership in the 90s was more managing expectations in an era of growth and now it's managing ... vested interests.
>
> It's a battle between those who say, 'We have to accept this new framework and tackle the interests which are holding us back,' and those who are saying, 'No, all we have to do is keep doing whatever we were doing so we can go back to where we were'.
>
> I don't think we can ever go back to where we were.

To address any one of the social and economic challenges that we face requires bringing a range of diverse interests, values and beliefs to the table and to work in a way for which we haven't been trained or prepared. No-one has taught us how to really work across difference. Yet engaging with this difference is the key to the co-creation of something new. We have an opportunity to use and integrate the strengths that Australia's diversity brings.

> ... where the parties develop a willingness to enhance each other's capacity for mutual benefit and common purpose, collaboration occurs. Here the parties share risks, responsibilities and rewards; they have high levels of trust, large time commitments and they share turf.[2]

This is commonly called collaboration. We are intentionally using the term 'leading across difference' to highlight the challenge and the opportunity that lies at the heart of collaboration. When collaboration works well it draws on the uniqueness that each party brings to it. Acknowledging and leveraging difference and diversity, rather than ignoring it, gives way to new thinking built on the energy of difference. This involves being open to discovery, while appreciating and challenging our thinking about leadership practice.

To work across difference in this way is transpersonal. It generates many more ideas beyond our self-interest. It requires a willingness to drop being wedded to a particular approach, to be wrong, to be vulnerable and to be ready to give something up. This is not what comes to mind when most people think of 'collaboration'; it requires an ability to assess and build trust with our collaborators. Ultimately it involves having compassion for others.

To maximise our ability to lead across difference we need to know why so many collaborations fail. The easy answer is that we had the wrong people, poor timing or insufficient resources. These are important factors but they are only part of the answer.

The 'seduction' of collaborating

Collaboration is a seductive idea. Government departments actively encourage NGOs (non-government organisations) to work in collaboration to achieve more sustainable outcomes. NGOs espouse the benefits of collaborative practice and business is starting to talk about the need for more collaboration with the communities and customers they serve.

This may be part of the answer. Yet the reality is often that the majority of leadership initiatives that require and espouse working collaboratively fail. This failure is partly due to the fact that not all challenges require collaboration. Sometimes, collaborating makes things worse. Expectations are raised and people end up disillusioned and disappointed. Often what is required is for those in authority to make a decision, but unfortunately collaboration can be used as a way to avoid taking this responsibility. It can allow us to avoid making tough decisions or having conflict. It is not a panacea. Most of what organisations strive to achieve is, and should be, done alone.[3]

Knowing when progress requires a collaborative response requires us to first understand whether the problem is 'adaptive' or 'technical':

- **A technical challenge**—Is the problem relatively well defined and you currently have the resources and thinking to tackle it by yourself? Or can you bring in the specific skills and capacities to tackle it with you? If the answer to these questions is yes, the problem may require coordination but not necessarily collaboration.
- **An adaptive challenge**—Is there a high level of complexity where numerous approaches have been tried and the answer is still unknown? Does no single entity have the resources or authority to make the required change? Does making progress depend on the whole system being able to work with people, organisations and communities who hold different views, beliefs and ideas? If the answer is yes to one or all of these questions, then this problem requires collaboration.

Collaboration is not a goal in itself: it is required when the system as a whole has to find a way to think and work *together* to make progress. It seems like we have the same romantic thinking about collaboration as we do about another cross-stakeholder venture: marriage.

In marrying another we believe, or at least hope, that the unity or joining together will always produce something good and create a better life than the one we could have on our own. Yet the sad reality is that one in three marriages end up in divorce in Australia. Collaboration, like marriage, takes us to the edge of our competence: we need to learn new ways, give up a few things and compromise to make it work. Leading across difference, also like marriage, requires us to step into the unknown. And while the newness can be exhilarating, once the romance wears off we have to get to know people in a more real and honest way.

Collaboration often brings us together with people we haven't worked with before. Even if we know them, new challenges are going to bring out different roles, approaches, allegiances and values. We don't know what's going to happen and we don't know how the other parties are going to respond. This point of ambiguity is where collaboration often fails. When we can accept this uncertainty, new possibilities often open up. As CEO of United Way, Doug Taylor, describes:

> In my role I'm meeting with boards and other CEOs. I realise that they often don't know what to do either. There's something very motivating in that . . . because they're the people you would *expect* to know. That's given me huge confidence because I've come to the conclusion that if everyone else is struggling, then why don't I take the lead? I often tell people I don't know what to do, that we're making it up as we go along and it gives us extraordinary freedom.

While this kind of freedom is enticing, it is not easy. It brings forward a number of traps which can kill collaborative efforts before they get too far. We call these traps the 'three Cs of collaborating': *competition*, *control* and *commitment*.

Competition

Motives and agendas of people are inevitably diverse. Stakeholders in any system are often in unspoken competition for resources, authority, recognition or power. That's just on the surface. Underlying we also have competing values and interests that demand to be maintained or looked after.

For example, in the corporate sector, organisations often have unspoken factions that align according to whose needs are most important to serve: shareholders, employees, customers or the greater community. It's not surprising that marketing, human resources and finance departments often find it so hard to speak the same language let alone collaborate. And that's just within the organisation—these 'competitions' become amplified beyond the organisation's borders.

In the community sector, organisations are often in overtly competitive tendering processes for government funding, yet are also required to work together to deliver services that benefit clients. And when they're working for the 'greater good' competition becomes a dirty word.

In the government sector, most federal policy reforms require both cross-departmental and cross-sector collaboration. With functional silos so common, leading across a department's boundaries requires change agents to have increasing agility in looking past their own functional interests to the broader departmental and systemic purpose and goals.

Competition is inevitable when different values and beliefs are being negotiated. Yet it is often not the competition that gets us stuck, but the silence and difficulty we have in acknowledging when, and with whom, we are in competition. This silence is a result of our challenge in acknowledging the different levels of power and resources that we all bring to the table. It means that those with less power and resources can feel unappreciated, devalued, and consciously or unconsciously end up blocking progress. The result is often unspoken competition for whatever power is available.

Collaboration requires us to understand, bring to the surface and speak to the underlying values and potential fears that are really at the heart of making change or progress. It can help progress if we are also able to 'get skin in the game' by showing that not only do we understand what's at stake, but are also willing to give up something to make progress. As Richard Sennett states in *Together*: 'By its very nature, competition breeds resistance, since the loser doesn't want to lose. Competition must embrace the losers' share in this exchange.'[4]

To be able to work with competition in collaboration we need to firstly be able to work with it in ourselves. We often deny this trait in ourselves and project it on to others. Yet, the gift of competition is that it also represents positive values—including survival, care for our family, community or tribe, a desire for progress and an interest in learning. These are useful values to bring to any collaboration if we appreciate, accept and know how to use our own competitiveness.

Control

Leading across difference requires us to let go of full control of what's going to happen and how it may happen. This can be a hard gig, particularly when we are used to having power, being in control and looking competent. For example, it can be hard for government when collaborating with the community sector to genuinely enter a creative space and let go of the 'master and servant' relationship they may hold.

Levels of power and authority are always unequal in collaboration. When we feel we have less power and are undervalued or unacknowledged, we hang on to what we have in the power and resources stakes. If we are struggling to trust our partners in the collaboration and feel we need to better compete, we may believe we stand to lose something and hold on to what we have a bit more tightly. Alternatively, if we are used to being the dominant partner in a collaboration then we may fear losing our power to others.

The tighter we hold on to what we have or know, the harder it is for us to innovate, take risks, and be open to difference and diversity.

> Employees want to keep information and expertise to themselves often because of a fear of becoming less valuable if their knowledge and expertise is shared by others: a 'knowledge is power' attitude. Helping others within the organisation can often be a low priority and sometimes people are just afraid of being embarrassed by sharing a creative or whacky idea to solve a colleague's problem.[5]

Commitment

It is highly unusual for a collaborative venture to have all parties with equal motivation and levels of commitment. There are always competing commitments, but in and of themselves these are not the problem. It is when competing commitments are unacknowledged or misunderstood that they can immobilise or block progress.

Surfacing these differences challenges the assumption that we are equal collaborators in terms of commitment and effort. This inevitably brings some level of conflict. Many collaborations fail when people believe, often rightly, that they have more commitment to the outcome than other stakeholders. This might manifest in stakeholders failing to deliver on what they've committed to do. So one stakeholder may just take over and others might be accused of not pulling their weight.

Often stakeholders don't commit to creating the right processes to allow adaptive collaboration to happen in the first place. In other words, we want to work differently together but use the same approaches that are designed to maintain the status quo. We get halfway through the work of collaboration and realise we didn't really put enough resources, time and thinking into enabling us to work differently and creatively. A new learning space is needed for collaborations to be successfully adaptive, to shift thinking and to co-create the new solutions required. We call this the creation of a holding environment (to be discussed in Chapter 12).

What is required to lead across difference?

Leading across difference is the primary work of leadership. With a greater awareness of what traps we can fall into through the paradoxes of Australian leadership, we now move to exploring what skills are required to collaborate successfully. Generally, the skills we think are required tend to be technical; having the right structures in place, with clear goals and processes, is important. However, the main skills needed to sustain collaborations are predominantly interpersonal, not technical. Namely, our self-awareness and how we work with others are crucial elements in successful collaboration. Our ability to be open, explore possibilities, hear different views, empathise and experiment tend to make the difference between whether we succeed or not.

A 2012 study of senior managers in the US public service[6] found that the defining characteristic of successful collaborators was interpersonal skills as opposed to technical expertise: 'Contrary to expectations, the federal executives most frequently mentioned individual attributes and interpersonal skills as essential for successful collaboration, followed by group process skills, strategic leadership skills, and substantive/technical expertise.'

In our work with thousands of change agents in the corporate, government and community sectors, we have seen people exercising a combination of skill and awareness that facilitates leading across difference. The next chapters offer more detail about the skills that enable us to shift the way we think about and practise leadership in Australia. They are the 'how to' of leading across difference. In these chapters we address the challenges and opportunities presented by the paradoxes of leading in Australia.

First we need to know **why before how**. Chapter 9 puts forward the importance of a clear collective purpose that is aspirational, achievable and galvanising.

Chapter 10 explores how we use our **power, rank and authority** to realise our purpose. To lead across difference we need to understand the power that we have at our disposal. This chapter describes what power looks like in effective leadership and further explores how to utilise the different types of rank that our power gives us. We examine what happens when we are not aware of the rank that we have and the impact this has in thinking about and changing our leadership practice.

Confusion and blurred boundaries between self and role are common obstacles in making progress, particularly in Australia.

Knowing how to *find*, *make* and *take* our role are skills that we can develop. Chapter 11 explores the range of roles that can emerge when leading across difference and outlines the awareness required to occupy the role of leadership.

Innovation emerges when diversity is harnessed to co-create new solutions. With this diversity comes conflict. The subject of Chapter 12 is knowing how to harness the potential of ***conflict to promote growth and innovation***.

We have outlined how our Australian story on authority is always influencing the kind of relationship we develop with those above us. It also influences the way we take up the role of authority ourselves. One of the main sources of conflict arises when we try to negotiate with the authority role. Chapters 13 and 14 explore ***why*** and ***how to do business with authority***.

We reflect on how to ***do more than survive*** in Chapter 15. The enticements and seductions of leading can often divert us from the reason we are trying to have an impact in the world. If we want to improve the world around us, we have to start with ourselves.

Finally, we call for a new story about Australian leadership in Chapter 16, one where we leverage the opportunity of the paradoxes.

CHAPTER 9

LEADING IN AUSTRALIA— THE WHY BEFORE THE HOW

To know how to free oneself is nothing. The arduous thing is to know what to do with one's freedom.

ANDRE GIDE

The vision thing

The vision for Australian leadership we are trying to bring forward in this book has been both explicit and under the surface. The first part of the vision is that leadership has a positive social impact—regardless of where it is practised or by whom. This means that we can look back and see that our actions have over time made our whole system, not just one part of it, better off. Leadership then is assessed not just in terms of our economic growth but in terms of fairness, inclusion and sustainability. If it doesn't have a positive social impact, it isn't leadership.

The second part of the vision is that if Australian leadership is going to shift, Australians need to play a central part in that.

This may sound like stating the obvious. It isn't. The responsibility for how Australia's leadership is practised, modelled and represented is, in our experience, not something that even those with a lot of power and influence often think about. It means that if Australian leadership is going to improve and reach its potential, all Australians who are interested in having a positive impact are tied to its improvement or demise.

This has important implications. It means that everyone with formal and informal power and influence has the opportunity to inform and alter the story of leadership in Australia: that it impacts all those around us and those after us. It won't come from spectating, commenting and complaining but from participation in its improvement. This participation looks like progress being made on our toughest issues and biggest opportunities by people working across difference and solving their own problems.

It requires people coming together on issues that are important to them and their organisations and communities, uniting in a shared purpose and starting the work of co-creating a better future, *not* waiting for the fantasy leader to arrive who can solve our problems.

So who writes this leadership story? It is not only those in positions of power with high public profiles who can write and tell the story of leadership in Australia. It is all Australians. The most powerful may actually have the least influence on the story because of the expectations on their roles to maintain the status quo.

What we do every day *is* the story of leadership in Australia whether we like that linkage or not.

The third part of the vision is that Australia can use its privilege to model and practise leadership in the world beyond our shores. In how we lead we can show what it means to create a society, community and organisations that are fair, inclusive and resilient. We can show that leadership can be positive and not just the focus of our complaint. In this part of the vision Australia can occupy a place in the world that can galvanise others to lead differently and learn about an alternate and better reality. The world needs more than just a conceptual idea of what a better society can look like. It needs to see it modelled.

This vision of Australia is perhaps more shared than we think. And it's not partisan, sectoral or geographically bound. It exists within the conservatives in the centre of power as much as it does within the progressives advocating for change on the edge of the system.

> And no society which values frankness and civility as national character traits can feel comfortable with the almost unparalleled level of public cynicism and disbelief towards the pronouncements of many of our political figures.
>
> We can prevent suffering from turning into despair; we can provide the human idealism and faith needed in the modern world; and we can ensure that the human capabilities of our people are fully realised.
>
> Former prime minister John Howard, Headland Speeches, 1995[1]

> A nation that better reflects the generosity of spirit, innate sense of fairness, strong community pride and ever-ready humour of its people. A nation that does not shrink-back and buy into fear or division. A nation unafraid to aim higher and to understand its place in the world.
>
> Simon Sheikh, former national director, GetUp, 2012[2]

In the current turmoil and disruption of the 'old world' paradigms of Europe and the United States, there is a glimmer of an opportunity for something else. The world appears to be calling for new forms of collective action, where leadership is exercised with transparency and fairness. Australia has more room to move than many countries. Can we seize the moment and start modelling a new approach to solving our problems, or do we continue with the same old song?

A call to action: Why bother?

What does a 'call to action' look like? The leap from dissatisfaction with the current reality to *just doing something* is unfortunately far too common. We see how far relying on dissatisfaction as a purpose gets you when we look at our struggle to know what to do on issues such as climate change and refugees. The omission of a clear and compelling purpose is the reason why so many change initiatives fail, no doubt feeding our disappointment in leadership in ourselves and others. This omission is understandable. Asking *where* and *why* questions can be much more destabilising because:

- They force us to think about our personal purpose.
- We are denied the immediate gratification of launching into action.
- We have to think more deeply about what it is we want—not just what we don't want and what we don't know?

These are hard questions for us, personally and collectively, as once we start to explore what our collective purpose is, we have to deal with each other's differences. An unclear sense of purpose makes this kind of leadership almost impossible.

As we work on developing a collective purpose, it is wise to be cautious of being romanced by enticing visions. Indeed our disappointment with leadership is often because of the difference between what we espouse and what we do. We have all been seduced by grand visions of the future in our organisations, communities and politics. It can be difficult to admit that in the face of these visions we are concerned about our own loss and protection.

So telling Australians to exercise better leadership because it is the right thing for the nation probably isn't going to get us that far. This is the case particularly when doing the right thing might mean potential personal loss of power or competence or the creation of a high level of uncertainty. It is not enough to know that others do not have it as good as us globally or that this is the case even here in Australia. Guilt is also a non-starter. Nor is our privilege a motivator in itself. The privilege we have is not a motivator if most Australians don't even recognise that we are privileged. Acting from guilt or privilege is not sustainable or motivating. Our actions can become short-lived when there is no quick payback for our ego or relief from our guilt.

Additionally, at a national level, Australia has no broadly felt crisis that would motivate a different type of leadership. Even so, global experience tells us that crisis doesn't generate much long-term change in leadership. It can act as a catalyst, a momentary disruption of the status quo, which if seized can result in change in the short term. While the fall of the Berlin Wall, the end of Apartheid and the Arab Spring all brought hope, over the longer term a fairly traditional practice of leadership remains.

If we focus on the individual benefits of exercising leadership, in other words our own self-interest, there might be more traction and staying power. This is another way of thinking about self-interest which benefits more than the individual.

In this book we are advocating the self-interest of living and leading to some kind of purpose. In our experience working with leaders across Australia, one of the most destabilising (and, over time, energising) questions you can ask someone in a leadership position is 'What is your purpose?' This question often elicits a number of responses; perhaps with much more of a global and generous view than one might expect of those in leadership roles. They are commonly:

- To make the world a better place
- To leave a legacy for my family, community or organisation
- To live a happy life
- To give back to the world
- To bring what I am good at to the world.

These are important and sustaining views that unfortunately rarely surface in our life in systems. They are not only *not* talked about, but often there is no linkage between these hopes of a purposeful life and the roles leaders occupy in organisations. We are not advocating that our systems should be dominated by each leader's personal purpose but that we are able to use what comes with our purpose to drive progress, hold a higher dream and use our own energy and resilience.

Systems with leaders who are unclear on their purpose easily get caught in the doing, get led astray from initial intention, resort to technical fixes in the face of complex challenges, and often end up with unspoken competition on individual agendas. As we lead and experiment we need purpose to orientate and sustain us—sometimes that is all we can be clear on.

The potential for Australian leadership is to connect power to a desire for purpose in our lives, organisations and communities. Reverend Tim Costello, CEO of World Vision Australia, expresses both the negative repercussions when purpose is not accessed in leading, as well as its untapped potential:

I think it's fair to say there's a fairly poor universal view of CEOs. But I don't think many go out the front door each day saying: 'I don't care. I'm heartless. I'll just screw everyone over to get the company bottom line up.' On the contrary, I've found the great majority want to do good. The hard part is helping them find a way to do good that's still consistent with their CEO and financial goals. In short, you have to help them find wriggle room.[3]

In this 'wriggle room' is where the energy and vision lie for everyone who is trying to exercise leadership. So what gets in the way of finding and using it?

The Great Australian Cringe

Thinking and particularly talking about personal purpose can be difficult. We worked with a group of senior leaders from the education sector who got very annoyed that we even asked the question about what their purpose was in their lives and roles. They assumed it was obvious. It wasn't. This is not uncommon. Our experience of working with people on their purpose is that it is difficult, inconvenient and sometimes annoying: they may need to question what they are doing and why they are doing it.

It can be unbearable to face the reality that we may not know why we're doing what we're doing or that it is unclear. Perhaps we have just 'found ourselves in this place' and never thought of why we were there. We may come up against our predisposition, skill and reward-structure of 'just doing'. We may also find that what we wanted to achieve in our roles is either not being met or is currently not possible within the place we find ourselves in. Can we face that reality?

This was one of the hardest chapters in this book to write. We found we repeatedly bumped up against not only the difficulty of examining purpose, but also our own cynicism. Our caution of getting too 'up ourselves' is a strong and grounding Australian trait. It is useful to keep us grounded, as long as it doesn't stop all action. But what does it disallow?

It is part of the human condition to strive for improvement and to make progress. This is how we have evolved. But as Australians we can be sceptical of this kind of personal agency and progress: we either want to mock the act of making progress or put it on an unattainable pedestal.

Perhaps we fear that if we own a higher purpose and dream, it won't be shared, others won't be willing to join us or, worst of all, we may not attain it. And is that at the crux of the cringe: a fear of making ourselves vulnerable and incompetent? If so, we can end up unconsciously undermining our attempts to work towards a higher purpose as we fight against the inevitable vulnerability it will require.

Our collective task is to hold our groundedness (rather than just cynicism) while at the same time giving our desire to live and lead purposefully enough room to breathe and grow. What we can bring to this question of our purpose in the world is perhaps two great Australian traits: when we convert our cynicism into realism and our courage to optimism, it may give us what we need to use our power and privilege purposefully—ruthless realism coupled with unfailing optimism.

CHAPTER 10

POWER, RANK AND AUTHORITY

I think it's a paradox of power that we are experts in the other person's power, but rather clueless about our own. I've seen over and over again conflict escalate because each party underestimates its own power and overestimates that of the other party. It's a chronic condition to use more firepower than we need, thinking we're the victims, or the ones in the lower position, even as the other side thinks the same.

JULIE DIAMOND, CO-FOUNDER, PROCESS WORK INSTITUTE[1]

Big dogs don't bark

It is easier to go to sleep at night with complaint rather than responsibility. The Australian anti-authority story is comfortable. It allows us to knock power and yet still be reliant on it. We know this story of the underdog well. It is a form of power that comes with a moral high ground. The underdog can judge those in power and their failures, inadequacies and (suspect) motivations and never have to take much responsibility. This kind of power is often adversarial and rigid—particularly in times of change. It can hold the power of not being committed. It's why the 'Whatever!'

response from teenagers can be so annoying. Showing we don't care is a way of keeping power to ourselves.

The underdog is a classic victim role. But victims can't operate on their own—they need tyrants. In fact they often inevitably create tyrants. The tyrant, just like the victim, has difficulties with owning their power and the inherent responsibilities. They have power and privilege but little understanding of its impact or potential. Liz reflected on this tension:

> I have right and history on my side. My own struggle in leadership as a woman carries a lot of history from my female forebears who have been strong, hard working women and a mother who has bucked the trend, fought against the tide and led change. I know the power that it brings—it's formidable. I've grown up using and seeing how this rank can either infuriate or immobilise others, usually men, but it doesn't always lead to progress.

Tyrants and victims are the two faces of an inability to use power. To make progress in leadership we are required to make the shift from tyrants and victims of power, to owning our power. Leadership then means shifting from using our power to fight against something or running rough shod over people, to using our power to create something.

When power, purpose and authority are linked, we have the potential to benefit the systems we work in and ultimately Australia. And without acknowledging and using authority (formal or informal) we not only risk abuse and neglect in systems, we can't make progress, either. This chapter focuses on the potential for change in our communities and organisations when we bring awareness to the power we have and skill to how we use it.

It can take a lifetime to grow into our power. As individuals few of us ever fully own our power—some not at all. As a nation we could say that Australia today is still in adolescence. Perhaps there was a more mature relationship to power before white settlement. Today as black and white Australians, we are still finding our way. If we can start to see that we have power and that it can be useful for all Australians, we might see that Australians are actually big dogs. And big dogs don't need to bark.

Using power

Leadership for a better world starts with us, our actions and how we live our lives. As one of the most stable countries in the world, we have a lot of power at our disposal. This doesn't mean we use our power well. For example, the gap between Indigenous and non-Indigenous Australians on most social and health wellbeing indicators remains significant; we have limited investment in innovation; and while we are one of the richest countries we are also the fifth most unequal in income distribution.

This position of stability and relative prosperity gives Australia significant power in relation to the rest of the world and with it the opportunity to use it well. But things change in systems one person at a time. For Australia to own and use its power well necessitates an understanding of our individual power first. And with Australia's strong egalitarian narrative, perhaps the most difficult bit is seeing and working with *relativities* in power—rank.

Understanding rank

Rank is the power that we have relative to one another in relationships, in groups, in the community and the world. Some we earn through the work we do and the experiences we have had in life. And some is unearned—we are born with it. As Australians we may hope and pretend that we are all equal, in reality we are always operating on an unequal and constantly shifting playing field. This message can be difficult to hear. And it is particularly difficult to hear for those with high rank who may have started life with low rank.

Rank is not something we can hide—although sometimes we may wish we could. We are identified and categorised by others through the signals we give (subtle and often unconsciously), how we communicate, our attitude, how we look, who we are with and what we might be sitting in (business or economy, Audi or Ford, Row AA or WX). This might sound like class but it isn't. Class is one part of a much richer array of elements of rank.

When we meet one another for the first time—whether we are male or female, black or white—our accent, how we speak and engage, our level of confidence and sense of place in the world conveys our rank. Most of us are aware of the areas in which we feel a *lack* of rank and are less aware of areas where we are rank*ful*. Ironically and most commonly, the *more* rank we have, the less aware we can be of how it affects others negatively. Arnold Mindell, founder of Process Orientated Psychology, talks about how people at the top of the ladder look down and only see the beautiful heads and faces of the people below them. On the other hand, those at the bottom look up and see only the backsides. People react to us as though we are aware of our rank—even if *we* are not.

Rank comes in a number of forms: positional, social, psychological and spiritual.[2] All rank is contextual: it changes dependent on where we are and who we are with, and is always only momentary. We notice how rank is temporary when we move to another context and are seen and valued differently or we value ourselves differently. For example, when we go from the office to the home environment. The four types of rank are explained below from the most context-dependent to the least.

Positional rank

The most context-dependent rank we can have is positional. This is rank that comes from positions we may occupy—like CEO, manager, teacher, politician, coach and parent. It is rank that doesn't transfer well from one context to another. This awkward transition is probably most easily understood by talking to male CEOs who humorously complain that their place in the hierarchy in the home setting is much lower than it is at work. This might explain the willingness to do such long hours at work—it's no fun losing all that power and status!

When we feel at ease, supported and respected in a certain setting, we have positional rank—but it is always temporary and context-dependent. This is perhaps why few ex–prime ministers have been able to build a successful career post-office—they seem to go into a lost zone where they get rolled out occasionally for opinion or support, rarely looking comfortable in their role. It is also what executives who are made redundant find the hardest in their transition to a new role or career. The sudden and unexpected job loss is most destabilising because they realise the significant power they had the day before has suddenly disappeared. People who were previously colleagues, subordinates and business contacts don't respond as willingly or at all to their calls or requests. They find out, quickly, how much of their power was positional.

Similarly, many immigrants who come to Australia face this same dilemma. With a new language and often without the positional rank of their previous profession to rely on, immigrants face a dramatic shift in their rank. Cultural enclaves in many of our major cities restore some semblance of rank in a new environment where recent arrivals have little.

As English becomes the world language, most Australians increasingly rarely have the opportunity to experience this grounding lesson in the transitory nature of power. There's nothing like not being understood to remind us of how context-dependent power is and how it impacts our sense of self. It is not unusual to hear Australians complain about travelling somewhere in the world where people *didn't* speak English. This is a complaint of the 'rank-blind', when we don't accept or see the rank we have.

Social rank

This is the rank we are born with and into. Social rank is like the air we breathe. Most of the time, none of us would stop and think about what power or privileges we possess that we did nothing to get. For example, before he opens his mouth or does anything, a white, English-speaking man in Australia will automatically be afforded certain privileges based on his gender, language and race. This is why this type of rank is often called 'unearned' rank. Social rank is based on factors like race, gender, nationality, sexual orientation, economic class, education, religion, age, health, physical ability and looks. In the Australian mainstream, those with the most social rank are:

- White
- Male
- Middle-aged
- Married with children
- Heterosexual

- Own their home
- Tertiary educated
- English speakers as a first language
- Brought up by two parents in their own home.

Like it or not, the more of these we possess the more we benefit from these privileges every day in ways that most of us are blind to. And this is where we often fail—because to use power well first we have to own it, not deny it or its impact.

As a white woman born in the UK, with university level education and professional experience, Liz's social rank allowed her to apply for and be granted residency in Australia in a very short time. Arriving in Australia, she was quickly welcomed into an established community. She understood the language (mostly) and was able to create an identity and life for herself quite easily. She could navigate the bureaucracies, apply for work, be interviewed and secure full-time employment at a management level within the first six months. Even her Scottish accent (which is clearly on the 'approved list') didn't get in her way: it gave her rank—in fact more than she would get in the UK.

This is not the experience for many others coming to Australia. But that didn't mean it was easy for Liz to accept her privileges. Our experience is that those with the most unearned rank either:

- Rail against accepting this power because it is (seen to be) unfair
- Are blind to or deny its existence—purposefully or not.

While this type of rank may be annoying to those that possess little of it, it is important to understand that with rank such as gender and race there are 'unearned' privileges that can be useful to making progress in leadership. We may not like this reality.

	Context-dependent/Low transferability
Positional rank	Rank that comes from a position within a specific system. For example: manager, government minister, parent, team captain or coach, CEO or school teacher.
Social rank (or 'unearned' rank)	Rank that we are born with or into. For example: race, gender, sexuality, education, lack of physical disability, culture, religion, age, language and marital status.
Psychological rank	Rank that comes from life experience. For example: self understanding and awareness, being loved and loving, feeling valued, having survived suffering and feeling stronger for it.
Spiritual rank	Rank that comes from being connected to something greater. For example: feeling or having something to offer the world and using it; having a spiritual practice; having faced significant loss, failure or trauma and survived; and having a 'calling'.
	Context-independent/High transferability

Adapted from Arnold Mindell, *Sitting in the Fire*, 1995.[3]

Psychological rank

This rank is acquired through life experience. It comes from many sources including:

- Being validated as a child
- Having loving parents or guardians
- Surviving suffering and coming out stronger and more compassionate
- Having attained higher levels of education
- Having self-awareness and a sense of knowing yourself.

In Geoff's work with teenagers early in his career, he noticed how easy it was to spot the kids from homes where they were loved and supported and adults believed in them. The general bluster and overconfidence of teenagers had a solid base for these kids—their confidence and self-efficacy was clearly higher. Psychological rank is tied to social rank—tied to race, culture, education, parents' education and where they grew up.

Psychological rank can also come from hardship as much as it can come from support and love. Victims of abuse and trauma or those who have survived great hardship also have a way of being in the world that is hard to miss. It is more than inspiring or heartbreaking—it's powerful. This power is often evident when white Australians are in the presence of Indigenous Australians—powerful white people can be sometimes overwhelmed, embarrassed or immobilised by the stories and experiences they hear. Their white, mainstream, social rank can get knocked out by the psychological rank of Indigenous experience and history.

One could argue that Australia as a whole holds psychological rank. Our confidence in both outlook and experience is hard to miss. Australia survived the global financial crisis and has had many years of prosperity, while the rest of the world has gone into recession: our way of life is one of the most enviable in the world. Moreover, Australians' egalitarian attitude projects a lack of fear of authority compared to, for example, our Asian neighbours. How we accept this rank and use it is part of both the opportunity and the challenge outlined in Chapter 5.

Spiritual rank

There is a certain power that comes from being connected to something greater than ourselves: a conviction or a belief. For example, while few Australians are practising Buddhists, the Dalai Lama's spiritual rank clearly has significant impact in turning him into a form of rockstar. This, in turn, gives rank to those who follow Buddhism. Priests also are often afforded an immediate rank within Australia, even among non-Christians. Their connection to spirituality places them in a separate category to everyone else. We see this with people referring immediately to them as 'Father'.

Spiritual rank can also apply to those who have had near-death experiences or faced immense difficulty that one could say has taken them to another realm of being. It is perhaps the combination of having survived suffering and become wiser from it, along with a connection to something bigger and unknown, which provides spiritual rank. This rank is also afforded to Holocaust survivors or people who have survived kidnappings or disasters against all odds.

As one of the oldest civilisations in the world, Australia's Indigenous culture has potentially significant spiritual rank. Indigenous elders are automatically afforded spiritual rank within their culture, and when they are with Indigenous Australians many non-Indigenous people can feel 'out-ranked' by their lack of connection to a spiritual story and history. Unfortunately, the lower social rank of Indigenous people in Australia can make accessing and owning the privileges of this rank challenging.

Owning or not owning rank

The temptation, particularly in Australia, is to try to hide rank. When people don't acknowledge their own position, it generally inflames those with less rank. Those with less power can become furious—usually without knowing why they are reacting in this way. With privilege it is difficult to consider how it feels to be without those advantages or powers. For example, many men are unaware of their sense of safety walking down a dark street, when many women may feel at risk. Or a person with white skin is unaware of the privilege of going shopping without being followed or suspected of being a thief, which many people of coloured skin experience.

So not seeing, acknowledging and using rank well can not only escalate or create conflict—it is tactically a big loss. It also means that the privilege isn't used. And the higher up we go the more useful we can be to our whole system—*if* we can accept our rank.

Abusing rank, what most people fear from others and perhaps themselves, is when the privileges are used for the benefit of one set of interests. Many have experienced and perpetrated this in some form with or without awareness. With or without intention, the effect is the same. This is why there is such sensitivity around the words 'power', 'rank' and 'authority' in Australia: power has not done itself many reputational favours over the last two centuries.

This makes it challenging, particularly with Australia's egalitarian values and anti-authority narrative, to become aware of rank, let alone accept the privileges that go with it. Yet with awareness of these privileges comes the possibility of using rank on behalf of others in organisations and communities—if we can see it or let ourselves see it.

> Jane works for a large Australian corporation. She is employed by the People and Culture division but sits 'in the business' as a senior manager responsible for a sales division. She reports to the division's general manager. She and her general manager are charged with implementing a new performance management system to lift performance. As the division struggles with change, she notices her (usually confident and

> unstoppable) GM seems to lack confidence with his staff in explaining the change. She also notices a continued deference to her. This disturbs Jane, particularly when it is done in public settings. At one meeting in front of his staff, he asks sheepishly, 'Am I explaining this correctly?'
>
> Jane comes to realise, slowly and reluctantly, how much rank she actually has in this division. Her initial assumption of having little, because of her gender in a male-dominated setting and her profession (from the 'fluffy' side of the business), is proven wrong; she didn't own the rank that came with her experience, technical skills, confidence and connections. As she starts to take ownership of this rank she becomes a more useful (and powerful) member of the division and begins to successfully drive the change she was hired to implement.

There is a lovely irony in the process of exercising leadership. Before anyone else can authorise us to act, before they can trust us or even follow us, we have to be able to authorise ourselves and see the rank we have to do that. It is easy to say, but can be very hard to do—at least with grace, compassion and magnanimity. Interestingly, in our experience, women seem to make this transition easier than men. Perhaps because they have felt more keenly the deficit of social rank in their gender and as a consequence are able to embrace and use their psychological rank more readily.

Without this awareness we not only don't take advantage of what's at our disposal to make change, but can also inflame others with less rank. What we may not see or be willing to see is obvious to everyone else.

Here's an example from our work: A group of white CEOs and other 'rankful' visitors are visiting north-west Australia. They are there at the invitation of a local Indigenous elder to discuss the planned development of a gas hub and its impacts on the region. Out of their familiar context and attire, they look awkward and uncomfortable. Over a number of days they experience a familiar dynamic for white visitors: an increasingly angry download on the state of Indigenous affairs and life in the region from the traditional owners. The visitors become quieter and more confused.

Yet while they feel powerless in their own eyes—that is not how they are seen. The more powerless they feel, the angrier and more virulent the download becomes from their hosts about the problems and what needs to be done. The visitors listen politely and leave tired and dispirited after two long days. An opportunity to use rank well becomes, instead, a sad dinner anecdote in a wealthy Sydney or Melbourne suburb.

In Australia there aren't many contexts of owning rank that are harder than this to deal with. We would go further and say that Australia's next generation of truly impactful leaders will be those who can own and use their power in the ongoing work of reconciliation between black and white Australia. The debilitation of the visitors is a natural response to feeling suddenly without their normal and obvious positional rank—as well as perhaps a dose of guilt. But what is often not understood is just because one may feel lower rank does not mean others see it that way. The Indigenous hosts could always see the rank of their visitors and became more inflamed with the CEOs' unwillingness to own this rank or do anything useful with it. The situation required an ability to stand in the heat of the moment and have a conversation without trying to disappear under a rock. The attack and download was only happening because of the visitors' rank, not because of an absence of rank. But that was difficult for the visitors to see.

It is dangerous to not own rank. But even when it is seen it can be debilitating. This can result in inaction when we tell ourselves we cannot do anything about the situation we're in. As well as being a waste of resources and privilege, it can also be painful. As Silas, a doctor and medical educator, reflected:

> I'm aware I have rank as a white male. I'm privately educated, a doctor, a teacher and now a father. I'm aware of my power but I'm often keen to avoid trading on it because it's too easy, it feels kind of cheap.
>
> I have antipathy towards authority—I reject the authority I know I embody, particularly as I start to get a bit grey. I keep rejecting it because I see authority foul things up and I'm keen not to repeat that. I have a desire to act at the same time as I'm pulling back from taking action.
>
> I see other senior managers pass up the ranks and I think I can offer as much as they can. But ambivalence is a comfortable, familiar place for me, I choose to sit in the middle of it although pulling back takes me nowhere. It's like purgatory. But nowhere's not a bad place.

Owning rank can be difficult to do, but the costs of not owning it are higher. The call to own rank from us as writers has, of course, an agenda in it—that Australians can use power to be useful for their systems and communities and not just for their self-advancement. It may have been possible in the past for Australians to stay in a bubble of power surrounded by like-minded and similarly ranked peers, but that is no longer an option. Australia has become more heterogeneous and power has become much more dispersed—we no longer have an option but to use our power more competently. If we can do this, it is in itself an act of compassion.

A battle for rank

Exercising leadership increasingly means transacting across very different levels and types of power. Our workplaces are more diverse, our society is changing and the world is getting smaller. To succeed we can't just do business within our own tribe—whether it's Indigenous leaders from remote Australia, whites educated in private schools or public servants in Canberra. There is rarely a full mandate or complete power to exercise leadership and make change. Indeed, all complex change is characterised by those in power not completely understanding how to make progress. Even if we did know the way forward we rarely have the full power to implement complex change. In this environment rank is changing and being contested all the time.

It is no fun being out-ranked. Even when rank is used with full consciousness and with good intentions, it will meet resistance. This can take many subtle and different forms:

- 'That's not how we do things here in . . .'
- 'We've tried that before.'
- 'Our organisation/profession is different.'
- 'That's culturally inappropriate.'

The usual way to think about these reactions is as a resistance or unwillingness to change. This immediately (and conveniently) casts those we are working with as 'resistors'. Another way to think about these reactions is that those we are trying to lead change with are reacting to our position and are threatened by it. We are also being reminded that our rank only goes so far. But perhaps, most importantly, we are being told that we have rank. There would be no reaction if there was no perceived rank difference.

This is an important point to remember because change agents rarely recognise and diagnose this resistance as an acknowledgement of their own rank. Nor do they see that the reaction by others to assert their own local rank is a way to restore personal power in the upheaval (and loss of power) created by the change. We can have some compassion to the reactions to our rank as a natural human response of others who are feeling their power and comfort being threatened.

This counter-rank pulling usually results in those trying to lead either backing down or running rough shod over the resistors in the system. Neither of these help progress. This is not owning or using rank well. Acknowledging that this counter-rank pulling is a reaction to more global status means there is more room to respond with grace, generosity and compassion.

Power and grace

If we as Australians can better own our power and use it well, it does not bring what we fear: arrogance, abuse or hubris. Rather, it brings grace and generosity. The journey is challenging for everyone, for those with more and less power alike. When we have power it may be difficult to see and admit to, especially if we have not used it so well in the past—either ignorantly or willfully. When we feel we have less power, we need to recognise the other types of rank we have—positional, psychological and spiritual—and see that we are not always 'one down' the ladder. Some of this work may mean letting go of a story about not having any power that has suited us well.

> Maurice is the director of a division that traditionally had been seen as marginal to the rest of the organisation. During meetings with his colleagues he found himself repeatedly in the role of either defending his division, critiquing the rest of the organisation or being the one to say no or disagree with everyone else. He, like all his colleagues, turned up to meetings advocating for their own part of the system. After feedback from a colleague about the potential power Maurice had in the group, he started to notice that he had a lot more rank than many of the others.
>
> He realised that his blindness to his own rank had led him to use too much 'firepower' in arguing his corner which, because of his power, led others to do the same. They were stuck with everyone advocating for their own needs, unable to see the needs and challenges of the whole system. As he worked more consciously with his rank, Maurice was able to start looking at the needs and opportunities for the entire organisation. The more he did this, the less he critiqued; and this allowed others to take up that role, too. He found he was able to model a way of working that benefited the whole system, enabling others to do the same.

Owning and using power is much more than awareness—it is a skill. It allows us to be not only useful but also compassionate and curious.

Worksheets

Exercise 1: Own and use rank more effectively

Write down the rank that you have in each of the four areas:

Positional	
Social	
Psychological	
Spiritual	

What privileges does your rank give you?

What might you do differently in your system with these privileges?

Get feedback from others about how you are using your power.

Exercise 2: Rank in conflict

In a conflict that you are currently experiencing, how might power and rank issues be inflaming it?

What would happen if you owned your rank more?

CHAPTER 11

THE LEVERAGE OF ROLE

Just as a role cannot be **given** to a person, neither can authority be given, it needs to be **taken** by the person in the appropriate role. All the trappings of authority are experienced by others as power unless this occurs.

BRUCE REED[1]

Who understands their role?

Understanding purpose and power are important to make progress, but they are not enough. It is easy to get caught between what the world expects people to do and a personal interpretation of what should be done.

What's missing is a way of leading that integrates who we are, the role we've signed up for and the context we're working in. We are more likely to be able to use our power to achieve our purpose in this middle place. This is where thinking about role is important but not in the way it is commonly talked about. Role is a widely used term, best known as the static and dead-end 'role descriptions' ascribed to a position in an organisation.

But role descriptions don't help people to innovate, prioritise or respond to changing circumstances. They become more meaningless higher up in a hierarchy, as the decisions that need to be made there are less clear-cut and almost always contested.

Role is what we do at the moment to moment intersection between us and the world around us (context). Some roles are linked to formal positions like boss or parent. Others are more informal—like critic, peacemaker or bully. Some are more permanent than others. For example, we can be a critic in a meeting but a brother or sister all of our lives. On any given day we cycle through many roles, sometimes just for a few seconds. Roles also coexist simultaneously.

Role is the middle place—not completely the context and not completely the person. For example, parents often face many opinions from many different sources on how they should be raising their children. They also have their own needs and desires (perhaps hoping to maintain the lifestyle they had pre-children). The role of the parent then, like many others, is stuffed full of expectations resulting in a set of overlapping and frequently competing behaviours. How we respond to these expectations and competing needs is constantly being shaped and refashioned at the intersection between ourselves and the needs and purpose of the system we are operating in.

Many roles are transpersonal, or as Carl Jung would say archetypal. People are pulled into archetypal roles because of who they are, their background, personality, preferences, needs and desires. The role utilises our uniquely personal traits and talents. This is why we sometimes find ourselves saying, 'That job is meant for me' or 'I was meant for this job'.

One of the foundations of a working society is the ability of its members to fill a multitude of roles—particularly formal ones.

As parents, spouses, partners and friends, we fulfil roles with and for each other. They facilitate survival and shape a response to the world and its changing conditions. Conversely, we see the impact of roles that are not taken up well. For example, when the role of parent is abused or misused, there is a devastating impact on children and society.

The more prescribed and established the role, the easier it is to take up. Leadership roles, on the other hand, are harder to take up well as they are more contested and open to interpretation. For example, everyone seems to have an opinion on what the prime minister or the CEO should be doing.

The need to understand and work with role is an important learning edge in Australia. The preference for informal relationships and the culture of mateship can keep Australians preoccupied with maintaining positive personal relationships. As a consequence working to be of benefit to the whole system may take a back seat to being liked. In addition, the ambivalence for authority can make it hard to take up the role of leader. The CEO of HiCAps, Simon Terry, describes this dilemma as, 'My stakeholders want me to be the bloke down the pub and King Solomon at the same time.'

The value of working more effectively with role is most easily seen and understood through its absence. One of the most obvious examples of this challenge can be seen in organisational life. It is particularly evident in larger organisations, and involves the most senior people. Based on their functional expertise and talents, senior executives rise through the ranks, then find themselves in a senior management group that ostensibly has a broader responsibility than just their prior functional portfolios: they are responsible for the health and sustainability of the whole system.

Yet very few senior teams are able to understand and grasp this new role well. This involves leaving their familiar functional portfolios behind so as to operate together as a group. A collaborative approach is needed to make progress in the system as a whole. While many organisations and CEOs long for a collaborative approach in their top teams—few understand the role shifts required to do this and hence the 'whole-system role' which takes a broader view is neglected. Instead, meetings at the senior level (having observed many of these as both managers and consultants) become stuck in protecting territory and reporting.

Neglect of this whole-system role is costly. It reinforces silos and blocks innovation. It can blind a system to external and internal threats and support poor funding decisions. While this is most intense and visible at the top, it is also a tendency that cascades down through most organisations. Only a small part of this challenge can be addressed through formal mechanisms such as job descriptions, KPIs and performance management.

So what makes a role?

Gavin was newly appointed as managing director of the Australian arm of an American healthcare company. Promoted from within, his new desk is 50 feet away from his old one. As he describes it, 'As I moved 50 feet I had to grow a bigger brain.' Perhaps it was not so much a bigger brain but a bigger understanding of what his new role required compared to his last. He quickly realised that the organisation's idea of what he should be doing was much more contested than he had previously thought. The less he defined it for himself, the more contested it became. 'In the first three months I just went from meeting to meeting,' Gavin says. 'I felt like I had no control over my time—my calendar just

> kept filling up.' Many staff expected Gavin to fill the role in the same way as previous leaders who had been much more centralist.
>
> Slowly Gavin also became aware of how his own personal preferences were influencing what he did. He recognised that his high detail orientation and desire to be involved in all decisions were not going to work: 'The big jump up was working out what I should leave behind and what new skills I needed to acquire.'
>
> Gavin explains: 'I have had to become much more self-aware in this role and understand who I am as a person before who I am as a title. I have had to define this role for myself before things went too far. I see the role now as primarily to protect our values and ensure we live by them—that and playing a collaboration and integration role between different stakeholder sets. Finally, also acknowledging that while it may not have complete authority, part of the role was to also take on the organisation's risk. One of the first things I did was take control of my diary again and then start to rewrite the script I was given. I actively refused to make decisions on high where I could avoid it (even though that's what many people wanted and were used to). I found I had to tune in much more closely to the rhythm of the organisation.'
>
> For Gavin, improved clarity and more congruent take-up of the role has meant that, 'My senior team has been able to make decisions that I couldn't have made and I was able to play a more useful role of championing it up the line, clearing barriers and facilitating change.' Some of that has meant a betrayal of old alliances in the organisation and letting go of an alliance with old, familiar roles.

As this case study shows, role is neither wholly based in context nor completely based in our identity as a person. It is partially both. Where they overlap is where energy, creativity and uniqueness enter the equation.

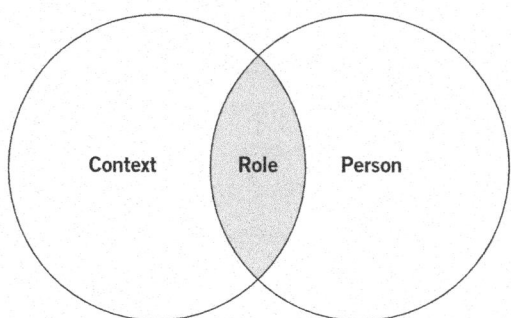

Adapted from Bruce Reed, *An Exploration of Role*[2]

The key to leveraging role is using the intersection between context and self as resources to *take up* a role and not be the victim of it. This means:

1. That there is no such thing as 'the right person for the job'. Rather there are people who assume a role that is effective for the context they are in and the purpose they are serving.
2. We may hope that we can get people to do a role—but as soon as it is conceived, part of the role will only be partially true as conditions are constantly changing. Instead, roles are always taken up by what people bring to them and what the context requires. Hopefully, we find a way into a role and, through making it our own, are effective in it.
3. There may be a gap between what the role and context require and the skills or awareness the person brings. This requires the capacity for the person to 'grow' into the role to serve the needs of the context.

Understanding the forces that impact on role

There are two strong forces at play in how we behave and orientate ourselves to the work of leadership: the force of the system we are

THE LEVERAGE OF ROLE

in at any one time, and the force of ourselves as people. These forces are both compelling and often invisible.

Role is constantly being shaped and refashioned on the intersection between context and the person. Neither the context or the person fully dictate the role. In the interaction of these two forces lies the challenge of understanding and taking up a role that serves the purpose of our systems.

The context

This is the myriad of circumstances that influence how a role is defined and taken up by a person. There are always multiple contexts playing out simultaneously. For example, we can be a peer and subordinate in the same meeting while also thinking about our children as a parent. Context is one of the strongest influences on role but cannot by itself prescribe it.

Visible context	Prescribed role (also called 'position')	Duties, functions, measures, tools and resources of a particular position.
	Position history	How the position has been taken up in the past by previous position holders.
	Consensus and contestability	The level to which a role is accepted in its current form and the competition for power within it e.g. perhaps the lowest consensus and most contested role is the prime minister's.
	Expectations on role	Culture, norms and what other roles expect of the role.
	Environment	Nature of the current context including level of urgency/crisis, built environment, economy.

Invisible context	Archetypes and fantasies	Models or ideas of particular roles that may be universally shared. Leadership often is the victim of multiple archetypes and fantasies that are not articulated. E.g. hero, nurturer, mother/father figure.
	Unspeakables	These are the sacred cows, cultural norms or expectations that a context cannot articulate or explain well. E.g., that conflict is taboo or that the boss speaks first.

The person

This is what we bring with us which impacts how we take up our role. These qualities are both visible to us and the world, but also invisible.

Visible person	Rank	The different forms of power we have particularly as they relate to others: positional, social, psychological and spiritual. (See Chapter 8.)
	Race, ethnicity, culture and gender	These areas impact not only our rank but also how we orientate ourselves to any particular context and role e.g. a person from a marginalised group may struggle to take up an authority role among their group.
	Ambitions and passions	Desires, ambitions, career goals e.g. Do I see this role as a vocation or a career stepping stone?
	Skills and life experiences	These dictate what we see and how we see it e.g. a HR background may mean we see most things as a people issue.

Invisible person	Personal patterns	Relationship to authority, preference for communication e.g. collaborative or individual approach; structure or process.
	Unspeakables	Desires, fears and longings e.g. Is the inner critic a strong voice within us?

> **Why work with roles?**
> Penny Ying-Yen Wong and Ian Elgin Macfarlane are quite the couple. She, a 41-year-old South Australian from the left of the Labor Party, born in Kota Kinabalu, Malaysia. He, a 54-year-old Liberal cocky from Kingaroy, Queensland. Yet ever since Opposition Leader Malcolm Turnbull gambled his leadership on negotiating with Labor to amend its emissions trading legislation before the Copenhagen climate summit, the pair have been spending long hours together trying to thrash out a deal. In an age where politics is more often played as a gory blood sport, could it be—God forbid—that Wong and Macfarlane actually quite like each other? They certainly seem to have a trusting professional relationship.[3]

This opinion piece brings to life the challenge Australia has in understanding how to conceive working relationships beyond the personal. Predictably, progress is seen to come from liking. The illustration for the article portrayed the pair naked and holding hands in the Garden of Eden. In interviewing Senator Wong for this book, her response to this article was quite simple: 'Well, we shared a mutuality of task.' What she meant by this was that the mutuality of task came from having a clear understanding of their shared purpose and their respective roles.

Using power with purpose

When roles are not taken up well, they can become dominated by either the context we are operating in or a personal agenda. When we dominate a role with our own agenda, it is easy to lose sight of the system we are trying to serve. This can be interpreted as greed, overambition and even passion. Role gives us a way to get on the balcony and see how our own personal needs for acknowledgement, being liked, being rewarded or the fulfilment of our values and desires are playing out. There have been many examples in Australian corporate life where people in senior positions have allowed their own desires for wealth and power to override the role they were serving to the great detriment of their organisations.

Similarly, in the community sector it is easy for personal passions and ideologies to dominate. The oft-cited critique of the community sector as lacking managerial skills is perhaps not so much a skill gap but rather an unwillingness of senior managers in these organisations to take up the role of the boss. Perhaps this is not where their passion lies or the reason they entered the sector in the first place. A symptom of roles being dominated by personal agendas is when we hear people say 'they are their role'. This easily leads to a misalignment of personal and systemic purpose. It is easy then for an organisation to get colonised by one or a number of powerful people's agendas and values.

As a focus on the personal can dominate a role, so too can the context. Systems make many demands and those demands become more varied and stronger higher up. As illustrated by the case study of Gavin, we may feel we are doing what's required of us, but that may not be the role that is best suited to the system's progress. The context can present many competing demands and in times of change will block as much as it encourages.

Role provides a way to put purpose first and foremost above the demands of both personal focus and contextual expectations. We can ask ourselves: *What is the role that is required here and am I acting in service of the system?* It allows us to use our power to make progress.

More than just friends—the Australian bit

There are dangers in judging the quality of our relations in terms of liking or disliking and getting on with or not getting on with others in the system. The first difficulty comes when we are unable to 'like' someone or get on with them, or when the needs of the business put our personal relationships under pressure. This means we might avoid sharing bad news or pushing across a boundary to preserve personal relations (Reed).

The other difficulty is it leaves us open to flattery, seductive enticement and collusion—intentional or unintentional. The role of authority inevitably gets positive feedback from its supporters or beneficiaries as much as it gets attacked from its opponents. Taking this feedback as personal can make us hungry for more and/or indebted to the contributors.

Bruce Reed, the late Australian expert on role, perhaps puts forward this challenge best:

> If I focus on my relations with others through our roles, we will not be preoccupied with getting to know them, cultivating personal relationships, whether I personally like or dislike them. I will be concerned rather with seeing my relations with them in terms of the task we are working at together. That is, recognising each other's roles. I will be aware that insofar as we are working at the same task we are doing something on behalf of each other, even if we disagree. To the extent that we acknowledge the same

task, we are free to disagree, challenge and be challenged, become angry, without fearing we will prejudice a personal relationship; or feeling guilty, because we accept that the criterion for what we say or do is whether it advances the task we are working at together. We are also open to being proved wrong in the process.[4]

Because there are dangers of an overly personal and relational focus, it is easy to swing to the other extreme—seeing relationships with people as purely functional and goal-driven. Similarly, this is just as problematic. One executive to whom we consulted felt his tendency to swing to this more transactional extreme for fear of compromising his role was logical. Unfortunately, it often left people cold and alienated. It was too far from the norm and didn't speak to the human needs we have of being in relationship, to be liked and valued at a personal level. Indeed, when this was brought to his attention by one of his staff, he realised that he didn't like being treated this way, either—it left him feeling like an undervalued cog. It was also too counter-cultural to work in this way. We can't ignore the Australian context.

What is missing is how to hold the 'and'. That is, the personal *and* the role. But thinking in terms of role may help here. Role can be used to clarify blurred lines between personal (others and ours) and the system's interests. We can see that, 'Yes, we are friends or colleagues or like each other or not, but in this moment I am in this role and you are in that role'. We can orientate our personal relationships to the purpose we're operating in. We can focus on our 'mutuality of task' and support each other's roles.

Resilience and safety

It is very difficult to hold senior and high-responsibility positions and be effective in them for any amount of time without a good distinction between self and role. The scrutiny, projections and critique of these roles are just too large to take things too personally. One only needs to check any daily newspaper to see the kind of scrutiny government ministers and CEOs face.

Clarity of role helps to manage and understand feedback, and particularly attack from the system, in a different way. Hearing attack from a personal frame is harder to deal with and also harder to transform. It is more useful to begin thinking about the feedback from a role perspective rather than just the personal. It is easier to shift a role than who we are as people.

The management writer Peter Block puts it this way: 'Take nothing personally before 6 p.m.'[5] After 6 p.m. there's an opportunity to think about the personal bit of some of the feedback we are getting from the system around us. It takes discipline and focus not to succumb and take the easier route of getting hurt or indignant.

There is much to be learned from prime ministers on the distinction between role and self. Indeed, one could argue that you don't get to be PM without a good understanding of role. A now famous interview of Prime Minister Gillard on the *7.30 Report* by Chris Ullman in May 2012 is an example of how to maintain role. Most notably this interview took place on a good-news day. Like many prime ministers before her, Gillard faced intense scrutiny and critique. Her treatment on the show brought a wave of criticism and an ex–prime minister to comment on its brutality. Also, like many prime ministers before her, Gillard was able to hold her role and not succumb or react to what must have felt like a very personally difficult interview.

A clear orientation to role also keeps everyone safe. Power is seductive. Everyone has desires and needs which can be easier to fulfil with the help of powerful positions. Distinguishing between personal needs and role needs can help keep systems safe and functioning.

Authority, leadership and roles

In trying to exercise leadership, the expression of the role of authority is the most important role to understand. Authority is a necessary part of exercising leadership as it gets people to pay attention, holds them in a space where some work can happen and can direct resources to the work of the system. This doesn't always require a formal role of authority but it does require power or informal authority.

Focusing on the role of authority is also doubly important in Australia. As discussed earlier, authority is a role that is central to many of the paradoxes of leading in Australia. It represents the greatest challenge but also the greatest opportunity. There is a chance to rewrite the script of authority in Australia with a clearer and more useful depiction of roles. The way previous 'actors' have expressed the role of authority in Australia has not done it many favours.

This section looks at the expression of the role of authority in two ways. Firstly, we present what is required for authority to fulfil its basic functions (also called technical work; see Chapter 2). Technical work is important in making systems function to maintain their current effectiveness. Secondly, how do these same functions look when adaptive work is required? This is where we need to go beyond the status quo to make change. It is tempting to be overly interested in this second area, but they are presented here as equally important. In our experience with many senior and experienced leaders, getting the technical bit right is 90 per cent of the work. Not only can we not begin to contemplate leadership without fulfilling the basic functions of authority, but most of the dilemmas in organisations and communities are a result of this technical role not being properly filled. The ambivalence to authority in Australia is so strong perhaps because the basic role of authority has so often been abdicated or abused. Simon Sheikh, former director of GetUp, reflected:

> I came in thinking this was a highly agile nimble environment which would lend itself well to being creative, provocative, free flowing. I thought the role would require me to get on with that and I was really comfortable in that space. What wasn't comfortable was realising that the context and the role were asking something very different of me. The organisation didn't know where it was heading in the future. The role of authority required me to build a safe space for the creativity to occur. That was the big learning for me because what it required was very traditional management: contracts, performance reviews, feedback and taking HR seriously. It felt at that time like it had nothing to do with what we were trying to do as an organisation. I felt uncomfortable because usually that kind of stuff requires experience (which I didn't have). It didn't matter that I was strong in other areas, the context needed something different.

The table below presents these two different roles in the context of a different set of tasks that are core to how authority provides *direction*, gives *protection* and maintains *order*. These functions are necessary in both technical and adaptive work but the role looks different in each one.

Role task	Technical role of authority (supporting the status quo)	Adaptive role of authority (exercising leadership)
Providing direction	Define the problem Provide the solutions and the way forward	Identify the challenge or opportunity Frame key questions
Giving protection	Protect the system and members from threats	Disclose external threats to the system to see and understand them
Maintaining order	Orientate people to their current roles and the relationship between roles Restore order in times of conflict Maintain and promote the system's norms	Disorientate current roles to allow adaptation and resist reorientation too quickly Expose conflict and let it emerge to promote innovation Challenge norms or support scrutiny of norms

Source: Adapted from the work of Ronald Heifetz and Marty Linsky at the Harvard Kennedy School[6]

Putting these different roles of authority into practice can look very different depending on who we are and the context that we are in. It is in itself an act of adaptation to make a role our own. And it rarely just happens without awareness.

Enriching a script: action with authenticity

> Acting is not about being someone different. It's finding the similarity in what is apparently different, then finding myself in there.
>
> Meryl Streep

The role of authority is a gateway to better leadership and a better status quo. To exercise useful leadership requires a clearer understanding and practice of the different types of authority roles and accompanying functions. The above table can sound like a prescription or a set script. In some ways it is a script. But a good actor always brings something of themselves that is unique and strong to a role. This is what brings a script to life. A poor actor either just reads the script or pays no attention to context. In other words, they just do their own thing without reference to the props, audience or other roles.

Sometimes the strength of a situation (or context) brings forth the role in people. In a crisis, for example, we see people emerge to do what is required, often with little experience or guidance. In the Queensland floods of 2011, premier Anna Bligh received accolades for the role she played. She demonstrated that she understood and could deliver on the core functions of authority to provide protection, direction and order. She also demonstrated her values were aligned with the people when she was able to show emotion at the lives and property that had been lost. In a crisis, the role of authority needs to be highly visible and to provide constant reassurance that order is in place. Premier Bligh did her job as authority competently and her approval rating soared—temporarily.

But this is not necessarily leadership. And as soon as the state got back to business as usual, its more complex and lasting challenges resurfaced. These challenges demanded a different type of role from those in authority. The situation wouldn't just create the role or provide the script. It had to be made and taken.

It can be disturbing to think that most of what we do is straight from a script—either the context's or ours. And the more authority we have, the more the context is writing the script. This is why a change in people in authority roles often doesn't make much difference to what happens in a system. Note how much continuity in actions and reactions there is between prime ministers and CEOs.

If we hope to be of benefit, rather than just a pawn in a system, then it requires awareness and action. The following approach developed by Bruce Reed[7] is a beginning to finding a better and more purposeful use of our power through roles. This is a process of *finding*, *making* and *taking* a role. To bring this process to life the role of school principal is used as an example—one that all people have experienced in some way.

Finding a role means firstly understanding the purpose the role can serve in the system. This might be different to what some of the stakeholders in the system are seeking. For example, some stakeholders are seeking continuity, others want their interests looked after, others are looking for a radical overhaul. In leading, identifying the clear purpose of the role can be hard to find but it is by far the most powerful part of 'finding'.

The school principal's question in finding role is: 'What really can this role achieve and why is it here right now?' This involves understanding the boundary of the role. For a principal it has traditionally been the school gates but increasingly today it is the wider community. The issues in the home and the community come into the classroom and principals find themselves having to hold multiple roles of social worker, parent or family mediator. In addition, schools are expected to meet increasingly stringent budgets while at the same time improving NAPLAN (National Assessment Program – Literacy and Numeracy) results. It means having a good understanding of all of the elements of the context outlined earlier and how these create a boundary for the role.

Making the role means adjusting the script to allow what is unique in us as people to come forward to match the distinct and current requirements. Education in the modern world requires experimentation and creative responses with insufficient resources. The making of the role here becomes the creation of an environment in which principals can engage teachers and the wider school community in a way that allows them to find their own answers and take up the role of community builder or entrepreneur themselves.

Taking a role may sound like the easiest part but can often be the hardest. It is where we authorise ourselves to fulfil the role and do what we think is most useful. It is how we start to behave to achieve our purpose.

Having progressed in their careers from their roles as teachers, principals are used to having all the answers and having a captive audience. Working in many modern schools requires them to take a role where they need to listen and negotiate in contexts where they have little formal power and need to often disrupt the status quo and experiment to find creative solutions. Taking their role means they need to move into areas such as management, where they might not be as competent, to allow new initiatives to emerge. This can be simple to *understand* and *make* but requires discipline, self-awareness and detachment to *take*. In many ways it is counterintuitive to the traditional role that the principal has occupied.

The criticism to this kind of approach of understanding and using role is most usually that of authenticity. That is, that this way of thinking and acting is inauthentic—it is not genuine—it is just playing a role. This criticism is partly valid—we *are* advocating playing a role. But we would argue that people are always playing roles. We usually do this with little awareness about who has made the role and how well that role is serving the purpose of the system.

However, there is a grain of truth that is worth preserving in the authenticity critique. It *is* important to be authentic as this builds trust. We can strive to be authentic to realise our purpose and bring our unique contribution to that purpose through the role—rather than just doing things our way, which is what we often mean by authenticity.

The Australian leadership role

Our organisations, communities and government are calling for people to take up roles better—particularly the expression of the role of authority. Leadership can become much more useful and resilient through better awareness and practice in this area. But while it is called for, it isn't necessarily immediately appreciated or wanted by those around us. There is a comfort in the status quo. Every executive and change agent knows that even though a community or organisation may want them to really own their role, when it actually happens it is not always that welcome. Inevitably there will be at least initial resistance to better take-up of role.

The opportunity, though, is broader than just local and organisational contexts—it is for Australians to express the role of authority differently in the world, showing what can happen when prosperity is used well, what it looks like to create a caring and inclusive nation and a just society. This role is waiting to be found and made. Australia brings something unique to this script beyond just our prosperity. We bring, through our relational way of doing business, a lighter touch. As Doug Taylor, CEO of United Way, reflected:

> It's interesting being in a global organisation and seeing how leadership is expressed so differently in other countries.

Australians are tiny fish in a big pond, but we carry a hell of a lot of influence relative to our size. I think it comes down to how we lead. I see CEOs from other countries really struggle to make change in a more collaborative environment that is cross-cultural—they're used to command and control. I got a lot of positive feedback about the way we work and how it's more effective and participatory. The phrase they use is 'leading from behind' which is such a contrast to the stereotypical corporate US style of an individual up the front telling you to go in this direction or you're out. My approach has been trying to find common ground to get the outcomes. It really crystallised for me how Australian leadership may be different.

Worksheets

Exercise 1: Understanding the forces which impact role

Step 1: Consider the role in which you are trying to exercise leadership. Map out the forces which impact the role in the context you are operating in and your own personal forces.

For example: Contextual force—Role requires me to sell.
Personal force—I'm good at implementing work, not selling it.

Visible context	Prescribed role (also called 'position')	
	Position history	
	Consensus and contestability	
	Expectations on role	
	Environment	
Invisible context	Archetypes and fantasies	
	Unspeakables	

Visible person	Rank	
	Race, ethnicity, culture and gender	
	Ambitions and passions	
	Skills and life experiences	

THE LEVERAGE OF ROLE

Invisible person	Personal patterns	
	Unspeakables	

Step 2: What emerges from this mapping about how you are currently taking up the role? Which forces are strongest? Which are least understood and need further exploration?

Exercise 2: Separating self from role

In the role in which you are attempting to exercise leadership, think of a situation where you are currently experiencing (or recently experienced) resistance or attack.

- How much of the resistance or attack might be about the role rather than you? What is it about the role that is generating this?
- How might the resistance be a function of how you are taking up that role? Are you being true to the role, or neglecting or abusing it?
- Which part of the resistance may be about what you are bringing to the role from your personal needs or interests?
- Is there another role that might be more useful in the system right now? How would you describe it?

Exercise 3: Finding, making and taking a role

With reference to the roles of authority on page 138, map the following process:

1. Finding—How would you describe the most useful role required to make progress on your leadership challenge right now?

2. Making—If you were to make this role your own, what unique personal strengths and experiences would you bring to it?
3. Taking—What would be required to take this role? What might you need to hold on to, or let go of? Where is personal innovation required?

CHAPTER 12

CONFLICT, GROWTH AND INNOVATION

Our work is here. We speak of power and of rank and authority, yet, beneath each issue, between the floating words and dissonance of opinion, there sits a fundamental opportunity for choice. Part loss, part gain. Our work is one of orchestrating dissonance, the ripples of which will alter the fabric of society, one conversation at a time. Some are soft, some are hard. All are necessary.

AN ADDRESS BY THE 2012 SYDNEY LEADERSHIP PROGRAM GRADUATES, SOCIAL LEADERSHIP AUSTRALIA, THE BENEVOLENT SOCIETY

It's all good?

It is easy to get excited about the idea of innovation. We hear about the need for it in our organisations and communities from political and organisational leaders alike. Most CEOs know that there are lots of great ideas in their organisations which could help their systems adapt and prosper. They also know that these ideas tend not to come to light or are quashed before they can get any traction. In a corporate organisation we worked with, the CEO lamented that a product improvement that would give them a leading edge over their competitor took more than six months to get any visibility at all in the organisation. What he found was that the system worked very hard to slow it down or kill it off before it got too far—often with the best intentions. It did this while promoting an organisational narrative of supporting creativity and risk-taking.

Innovation is a hope, slogan and call to action that often doesn't get very far. That's because innovation calls us to commit ourselves emotionally and psychologically. Hopefully, and necessarily, we do that with others who are making the same kind of commitment. If that can happen it inevitably means conflict with other ideas and interests—in fact, the resulting conflict is vital for the innovation. And this is where the hopes for innovation usually die.

We can't make a new year's resolution to eat and drink less, exercise more or quit smoking and not come into conflict with our current way of life, comforts and existing behaviours. Similarly, we can't find a way through some of Australia's adaptive challenges without similar conflict. Creating innovative organisations, responding to climate change, finding better ways to manage land and water, and tackling increasing obesity won't come without a clash of values, beliefs and assumptions between different interests in communities and organisations. Indeed these clashes exist within ourselves as individuals. Nobody *really* wants to get out of their comfort zone.

The clash or incompatibility between opinions, ideologies, beliefs or interests is what defines conflict. When it arises it is often a marker of where an individual or a system's growth is.

It's a bit like a road sign: 'Warning—Growth Ahead'. While it represents an emerging potential, we need to be prepared and skilled if we don't want to end up in the ditch or just turning around and going home.

Conflict is a tough sell in the Australian context—even the more positive interpretation offered here as a signal of growth. Not that it is necessarily easy anywhere else in the world or dealt with much better. We need only check out the international news to see how poorly differences between us as humans are dealt with. Yet there is something unique about conflict in Australia, both in how we deal with it and our understanding of its legitimacy in a peaceful nation.

While disagreements, differing points of view, tension and mistrust between groups and individuals are part of human existence, it is rare to see them openly surfaced in Australian workplaces or communities. Their suppression means that when and if they do arise they carry a lot more firepower than we were intending or they come out in a place where they cannot be understood and progressed. But before trying to understand why Australians struggle with productive conflict, it is worth understanding what it offers. Why would we want to disrupt the apparent peace? Because, as we like to say in Australia, 'It's all good,' isn't it?

Well, mostly. The space and distance from the world's troubles have been some of Australia's greatest assets. What was initially a curse for many early settlers has become one of our greatest opportunities. Beyond the material advantage, our space gives us the ability to relax and block out the world's problems. There's more than enough space for things to be out of sight and mind.

But as the world becomes both smaller and more diverse, it brings inevitable conflict. Australians are increasingly faced with a need to understand and negotiate across values, beliefs and interests. This is what we have earlier in this title called 'leading across difference'.

As Australians we can approach this with dread and anxiety or we can try to see its potential. The potential is the opportunity, indeed the necessity, to innovate. The ability to compete locally and globally is dependent on this. More importantly, communities and social systems are calling for innovation. Transport, child welfare, housing and an ageing population, to name just a few examples, are all calling for significant innovation.

Australia's prosperity provides a unique opportunity to be of benefit locally and globally. Are we willing to do something with this prosperity, knowing that this will inevitably involve some kind of conflict among us? This brings us to the Australian challenge—and opportunity—with conflict.

Australia and conflict

The paradoxes of leadership discussed in Part 2 paint a picture of what is unique in leading in Australia. A number of these paradoxes can inform some of the challenges with conflict and in turn innovation and growth: in particular Australian's relationship with authority, the preference for strong personal relationships (over task and role), and our egalitarian values.

Dependent on authority

Despite our irreverence, Australians show a high dependence on authority. When the status quo is challenged or called into question, this means we usually look to authority with an expectation that the role will fix or calm things. Often unwittingly those in authority will respond to this expectation by trying to move things on (away from the conflict), shut it down, 'put it in the parking lot' for later, blame the source of the conflict or resort to a technical fix. Easing the tension also helps maintain or restore authority, at least in the short term, because the expectations on the role of authority to keep the calm have been fulfilled.

At a round-table discussion on social innovation in Sydney hosted by a touring American academic, Geoff witnessed how easy it was for the innovation agenda to be pushed back to authority. As the conversation proceeded, the visiting academic repeatedly tried to explain how social innovation can only be owned by non-government players. Yet the Australians couldn't help seeing government as the central player and patron of any social innovation. The academic had missed the cultural difference between the two countries.

Anti-authority

The other side of the authority paradox is the anti-authority narrative or what might be more commonly called the 'larrikin spirit'. When we face difficulties and conflict, we not only look to authority figures to fix things—we can easily blame them. Authority can swiftly become the lightning rod for the problem. Instead of having the argument among us, we have it against authority. People in authority can be burdened with the problem, particularly if they do not alleviate the tension fast enough.

A police commissioner confided how difficult Mondays were in the police force following a weekend with a number of road deaths. The media and public seemed to see these deaths as the fault of police, a convenient home for it! This places the role of authority in a difficult spot. In times of change, authority's role is to alert systems to impending threats and challenges. In other words, they need to bring conflict *to* a system in order for it to respond differently and adapt (innovate), for which they may be blamed.

Preference for personal relationships

Australians display a preference for working with and maintaining strong personal relationships. In other words, 'being liked' is important (see box 'How to get ahead at work'). This makes it difficult to tolerate conflict because of a fear of being disliked and excluded. As a result, the more difficult conversations tend to happen outside of our formal meetings and usually with those that are 'on our side'. When the inevitable, and healthy, disagreement eventually gets some air, it is usually in the more comfortable informal context: in the corridors, down at the pub or at the coffee shop. It is a credit to our skills in working politically that we are able to deal with the undiscussables in this way. The downside is that it kills productive conflict that could help the system. It also reinforces the idea that difficult conversations are not sanctioned and need to be 'handled' somewhere else.

Many of us have experienced coming to a meeting where there was clearly a previous meeting to which we weren't invited, one where the majority got shored up and the decision was guaranteed without the danger of any messy disagreement or conflict.

Our personable, social approach, one of our greatest traits, becomes problematic when we *can't* just be mates, when something else is called for.

> **How to get ahead at work**
>
> Australians think the way to get ahead at work is to be popular with colleagues, while Brits favour the sucking-up-to-the-boss method. Germans think it's most important to dress the part and Singaporeans

emphasise being seen in all the right places. That is, according to research commissioned by LinkedIn and conducted by IPSOS Mori and Catalyst Research. The survey covered 3200 working professionals globally, including more than 400 in Australia. Three out of four (75 per cent) Australians rate being liked by colleagues as the most important factor in career development, the study suggests. This compares with fewer than two out of five (38 per cent) of the British respondents.[1]

AFR, November 2012

Egalitarian values

At least on the surface Australians hope for equality and sameness. Yet change often means that there are not going to be equal outcomes for everyone involved. In the face of this, it is easier to paper over the fact that some will benefit more and some may lose more, at least temporarily. Indeed any kind of real change will involve some kind of loss for everyone involved.

It is usually those who will gain more who try to do the papering over, as it can be uncomfortable to admit to and recognise another's loss. The risk is that we only hear the 'yes' voices that will benefit more from the change and not allow space for the 'no' voice that may lose more. We end up rewarding and creating an 'in group' and wonder why we cannot innovate. Papering things over in the hope of equality can make the conflict bigger and send it underground where it can't be used productively any more.

It feels strange to argue for more arguing, kind of like spoiling the party. But we often get stuck between two polarities. It seems that it's either 'all good' and 'no worries' or it's the high stakes, winner-takes-all scenes that we can see in parliament. These two scenarios are actually not that different. In one, conflict is buried, and in the other it is open but extreme. But they have the same outcome. Neither is able to really hear alternate voices or innovate. But why are these alternate voices, or the 'no', important in innovation?

The cult of 'yes' and the loss of 'no'—Why conflict is important for innovation

Looking to authority to fix or blame and fearing that conflict will jeopardise personal relationships means groups end up seeking a false and un-useful surface consensus. One senior public servant probably said it best to us in our research: 'We end up creating and maintaining cults of "yes" in our systems.'

Expressing 'no' then has little legitimacy or safety and gets pushed underground. As Leigh Weiss reflects:

> If I go to a meeting but don't have the chance to test my views against contrary opinions, I may leave the room saying 'yes' to initiatives without feeling any personal commitment to them.[2]

Where does this leave us if we are interested in innovating, change and growth? It leaves us sticking to the 'yes' and losing the wisdom of the 'no'.[3]

Sticking to 'yes'

The most obvious response to potential conflict is resorting to technical solutions (see Chapter 2). In an effort to avoid conflict, it is easy to revert to the known: restructuring, calling in consultants, setting up a working committee, running a consultation process, centralising, decentralising, or whatever the system is best at doing to turn down the heat. Technical solutions are also an implicit means of supporting authority. After all, technical work is the domain in which authority has the most expertise and is responsible for on a daily basis.

Authority is inevitably predisposed to look after the status quo and the interests of the majority or mainstream. Yet innovation and growth rarely come from the centre of systems. They come from the edges: structurally, geographically, culturally or ideologically.

These are the people at the coal-face hearing about customer or client experiences, those sitting in the regional offices or those who are treated or experience our systems very differently. These 'edges' have a different experience of systems to how the mainstream experiences it. They may be marginalised by the mainstream, alienated or completely overlooked. These edges often have unique perspectives and experiences of the systems we operate in, which often are the clues to a system's growth. But it is hard for authority and the mainstream to see and hear these alternate voices.

This often means that the 'no' voice ends up losing or alienated. This is not to say that loss should be avoided. It is very rare to have everyone completely 'onboard' and almost impossible for everyone to benefit equally in change, at least in the short term. The loss could be tangible (financial, control or security) or even just to our pride.

The dangers of losing the 'no'

Not allowing the conflict between parts of the system to surface and be understood, acknowledged and worked with has a number of dangers:

1. *We lose the wisdom* of those who are not agreeing with how things are or what's being proposed. The 'no' voices in systems are not objecting just for the sake of it or purely out of self-interest. They often represent a view which is useful to hear. The cult of 'yes' can mean losing this wisdom. For example,

an organisation we worked with was seeking to innovate in its service delivery to its clients. The 'no' voice raised the issue of how its managers treated its own people as a problem in this innovation—in effect it could not offer better services if it was harassing its own people. This was met higher up with disbelief or dismissed. Though difficult to hear, this wisdom was key to the innovation.

2. *Dealing with loss* is important and often underestimated. Those who are not benefiting equally or are losing from either the status quo or the proposed changes must deal with what it means to lose. The fear of admitting to or creating loss can mean that instead we do nothing and ignore it. In effect we don't know how to move on well.

3. *Creating 'terrorists'* is the other impact of not dealing with loss well. Ignoring the losses and just moving on is a great way to inflame people. It is no wonder then that change so often fails. Terrorists in mild forms appear in community and organisational life all the time. They can be identified by barbed jokes about the latest changes all the way to strikes and departures. Perhaps because there are so few opportunities for dissent to be voiced, we create mouthpieces for us to vent our frustration in the only way we know how. This might be why shock-jocks resonate so well with the disaffected. Perhaps our inability to hear alternate voices and deal with them well means we need to find other ways to be heard.

Conflict and the 'no' are valuable to making progress and growth. If we can't tolerate it, we end up creating terrorists in our systems. Terrorism can either be angry, loud and seeking to stop progress aggressively (which we usually leave to others to do for us) or the more passive and familiar resistance. In effect, conflict ends up polarising rather than helping innovation.

Thankfully Australians bring something to bear to this challenge.

Showing up—how to innovate

> People left by keeping their real feelings and thoughts ... to themselves preferring to support the friendly group atmosphere of camaraderie while gossiping privately about their views. In a sense they hadn't showed up yet.[4]

Innovation and change happen when people 'show up'. This means bringing all of ourselves into the challenges we face and allowing others to do the same. And when we show up we will inevitably meet some kind of conflict.

Australians bring significant gifts to the challenge of conflict: an awareness and sensitivity to the excessive use of power and an irreverence to authority. This 'naughtiness' is a good antidote to the cult of 'yes'. What's missing perhaps is the skill to do something with this naughtiness that allows progress to be made so it doesn't just turn into complaining.

Without these skills it is easy to get knocked out in the heat and confusion of conflict. The preceding chapters on purpose, role and power form the base of these skills. The following three sections outline what more is needed to use conflict productively from the perspective of purpose, power and role.

Purpose: productive conflict

Not all conflict is useful. Productive conflict, which is what this chapter is promoting, has a purpose of facilitating innovation. It does this by allowing a diversity of thinking to emerge. It has a fundamental premise that to reap the benefits people need to *stay in* relationship. Unproductive conflict, perhaps what we are most scared of, moves us out of relationships. It is highly emotive and divisive and drives people and interests apart. How do we make sure we are promoting and holding people in productive and functional relationships?

From positions of authority, we need to be ready to tolerate, contain and create productive conflict so that systems can innovate. This requires being able to develop, communicate and hold a clear and compelling purpose: one that is collective, positive, achievable, aspirational and galvanising. This may take some time to work out collectively. The questions about why we are doing what we are doing are usually not asked and groups can be months into collaborative work without being clear on why they are working together. Asking the questions about purpose and having to commit to a tangible outcome is challenging, but is authority's purpose. This compelling purpose can sustain a group through the heat of conflict.

Power to create a holding environment

Productive conflict requires the creation of spaces where conflict can safely arise. This is what is often called a 'holding environment', characterised by:

> The cohesive properties of a relationship or social system that serve to keep people engaged with one another in spite of the divisive forces generated by adaptive work.[5]

Holding environments enable groups to develop their identity while containing the conflict, chaos and confusion that is often produced when they struggle with complex problematic realities. This is like a pressure cooker to contain and regulate the heat. A pressure cooker, unlike a wok, holds in the heat, pressure and ingredients without a large flame. Similarly, in conflict it is easy to depart from a loose holding environment (a wok) because there are no barriers to exit or little incentive to stay, or because it is seen as too unsafe or too hot.

The majority of the work in innovation *is* the creation and maintenance of a strong and safe holding environment to keep stakeholders involved long enough to create something new and make progress. Unfortunately, what often happens in attempts at innovation is that, beyond the initial fanfare and sponsorship, there is little thought given to holding people in the work when it starts to get hard. So stakeholders stop 'showing up'.

A strong holding environment can create a space where a level of trust can be established to make it safe to bring forward difference. The harder the adaptive issue is and the innovation required, the stronger the holding environment needs to be.

The National Economic Summit held by the Hawke government in 1983 is a good example of the creation of a successful holding environment at a large system level. Coming to power months before, Bob Hawke created a strong container for the work his government was attempting. Using the mandate from the recent election, Hawke and his deputy, Paul Keating, assembled key stakeholders from unions and the business sector in a highly visible way, set a clear purpose and used the physical environment purposefully. The summit was held in the House of Representatives chamber with dinners at the Governor-General's residence and at the Lodge. 'For business chiefs the event was heavy with the smell of power and the weight of responsibility.'[6] The result was a commitment to wage restraint and support for the government's economic approach for the ensuing years: two feats that had eluded previous governments.

Good holding environments are critical in all types of difficult change and innovation, not just in systemic political change. It could be in a performance management process, product development initiative, inter-agency stakeholder meeting, or a team meeting. All of these instances, whether they are at the national level or one-on-one, rely on the judicious use of power to create a strong holding environment for the work to take place. Similar to the sides of a pressure cooker, power and rank can be used to create a holding environment where stakeholders feel safe enough to stay in the heat and not retreat.

But personal power is only one element of a holding environment. There are other tools, including the following.

Clear authority and sufficient structure

All collaborative efforts require someone to hold the authority role. This is the person or entity that can provide sufficient direction, protection and order for progress to happen. This is probably the most important element of a holding environment, yet it is tempting to shy away from the responsibility given Australians' wariness in owning power. Under pressure people will look to authority and seek safety from that role. People are watching so we need to be clear of our purpose and send out strong messages that 'we can contain this', which is different from just shutting conflict down. Using power well keeps people working and creating. Using power poorly means they will flee physically or mentally. There is nothing like a poor use of power to kill other people's intelligence.

Physical environment

Seating, location and room set-up can all help create a positive holding environment. If we are hoping for a different result from the same group of people, it might be difficult if they are meeting in the same place where they do their day-to-day work every week. We need to create new learning spaces if we want a new conversation where we can learn and turn up the heat.

Reputation and relationships

The expertise, practice and reputation of the stakeholders are important parts of a holding environment. These relationships develop with time spent together and the trust that has been built. If stakeholders perceive their collaborators and those in roles of authority can be trusted and are known to be effective in getting things done, it provides a strong holding environment to begin a collaborative and creative effort.

Existing culture

Bonds of affiliation between group members, norms and common values, traditions, language and rituals all can play a part in a holding environment. While the existing culture can impede change, it can also be used judiciously to support it.

Facilitation

Sometimes it is important to use external parties who may be more objective or neutral to free up stakeholders to work in the holding environment, particularly those in the roles of authority.

Time as a tool

In our work in innovation with groups and systems, it is no coincidence that the 'sticky' moments—where the group is able to have more difficult conversations—happen close to the time a session is finishing. Using time boundaries keeps the group focused on their intention and progress. Of course this needs to be balanced with creating enough time for real work to happen. Changing the way systems work takes time. Not expecting quick fixes and having realistic expectations are important.

Who's at the table

The more successful collaborations are often the more diverse and have the right level of mix and power in the room. The tendency is often to collaborate with people who are known and on the same page. That's fine with technical challenges, but for many of the adaptive systemic challenges in Australia, we don't get to pick the people we want to work with. Having people with a mix of skills, diversity of experience and world views is important when no one person has the answer or the authority to make change by themselves.

Experiences and familiarity with adaptive work and trust of authority

These are two important experiences that will determine how fast the group can move. If members of the group have no trust in authority and are not used to working more creatively, things will take longer. It doesn't mean these people should be excluded, it's just that the holding environment will take longer to build. As they are probably outside the mainstream, their voice is valuable: it will just require more thinking and awareness on the part of authority to make it safe for the group to learn and work.

Urgency

Create urgency in the environment or use what already exists to contextualise the work. Similar to Hawke's mandate, what's happening in the broader environment can play an important role in holding people. Is there a crisis happening or pending? Do people feel personal urgency from themselves or their sub-systems?

A new role: facilitating the 'no'

Innovation is one type of adaptation in a system. It requires authority to shift from its usual role. As discussed in Chapter 2 the role of authority is responsible for:

- Disclosing external threats—rather than just trying to fix them
- Disorientating people from set roles—rather than trying to keep people where they are
- Exposing conflict—rather than just shutting or cooling it down
- Challenging norms—rather than just maintaining them and supporting them.

On the one hand, authority needs to hold its role lightly enough to allow new developments to emerge, which will include conflict. And on the other hand, authority needs to ensure there is a strong enough holding environment to keep the heat up while making people feel safe (enough).

This requires more fluidity and lightness in the role of authority than is usual. It is a much more facilitative role: a 'broker of difference'. And this role can be taken up in both formal and informal roles of authority. It is required wherever there is conflict and can support a creative process that allows new ideas and ways of working to surface. How is that done?

- Through the skill of bringing forward alternate views (the 'no')
- By protecting the 'no' to understand the wisdom within it
- Holding steady during conflict
- Finding a way to not get stuck in the 'no'.

Bringing forward the 'no'

Authority is conditioned and supported to find 'yes': the mainstream view. This is the view that minimises and avoids conflict. Facilitating innovation and conflict requires a shift in how the purpose of the role role of authority is perceived. It requires what deep democracy practitioner Myrna Lewis calls getting 'inside the no' to help understand the wisdom of the alternate views.[7] Understanding the 'no' can also help to make decisions that stick; otherwise the 'no' will come back later in another form, usually to derail implementation.

'Deep democracy', originally developed by Arnie Mindell, is a process that focuses on the awareness of voices that are both mainstream and marginal. This chapter is based on some of its themes. It is an approach that can be useful to allow a more facilitative role of authority to emerge.

Firstly, it's important to make it safe to hear all the views and for disagreement to surface in the group or team. This unfortunately rarely happens. From the role of authority we might be the last person in the room to see how much we quell, disallow or ignore conflict and differing views. Often only the easiest view or the one that is favoured by the mainstream is heard. Usually the mainstream feels safe enough to advocate strongly for its view as if it's the only possible view rather than just another option. Unwittingly, the role of authority can cut off multiple and alternate views by how it asks questions. For example:

- Does anyone have a problem with this idea? (Translation: You might be the problem)
- Everyone agree? (Translation: I am not interested in who disagrees.)

Making it safe means inviting alternate views and modelling that it's okay for them to be surfaced. It can take time for groups to get used to this idea. They may not believe that it is actually okay to surface other views. We need to be prepared for silence, minimal contributions or an echoing of mainstream thinking, at least to begin with.

Another way of thinking of this is like a hunting exercise. Like hunting it requires silence and patience. If the clues to innovation in our systems were easily uncovered, they would have been found already. Alternate views often need time and coaxing to come forward. Authority's role is to keep waiting and asking:

- What other thoughts do we have?
- I am not sure we have everything here—what are we missing?
- What would an outsider say?
- What would one of our critics say?

Protecting the 'no'

The mainstream and authority have to work hard to hear the 'no' even when it does surface. We often hear from people in authority that they are interested in the alternate voices but are distressed that 'they' can't communicate in a civil or logical way, that the emotion needs to be taken out of the issue, or that normal channels and processes should be used. Or there is frustration, that the 'no' voice won't communicate at all. Assuming that alternate voices are going to sound like we would like them to sound, or make any sound at all, demonstrates a lack of understanding of how hard it is for these voices to emerge. For example, the reason the 'no' voice might sound so angry is that it may be the only way it can get heard. Systems are often not ready for alternate views and these people may have been burned before when they've voiced the 'no'.

The task is to protect the alternate voices for long enough to understand them and hear what wisdom they contain. This requires depersonalising views and ideas and ensuring that they all get protection. So, instead of asking 'Who else thinks this or feels like this?' (Translation: Do you dare to support this alternate view?), we could say, 'I think there's something in this (alternate view)—let's try to understand it more'.

And if no alternate view arises, it can be useful for authority to model it. For example, 'If we were to imagine someone who was against this proposal, what would that person say?'

Working in this way requires us to develop the skill of depersonalising ideas, hearing all the views and sitting with the conflict. Bringing forward alternate views is an interactive and intuitive art. It requires looking for the clues of dissent and then helping the group use them to form a range of interpretations about what might be going on and what is possible.

Holding the conflict

Roles of authority are always signalling what behaviour is acceptable and unacceptable. Systems are particularly sensitive to cues on conflict and disagreement. If authority consistently adopts the mainstream view without open debate and cannot hold and protect alternate views, others below are likely to follow that lead. On the other hand, if there is an open commitment to debate and an explicit understanding that debate moves the organisation to better decisions, then employees are more likely to bring their ideas into the arena.[8]

To work with conflict productively means taking on two critical assumptions about collaborating or 'working across difference'—that there is wisdom in the group and an acceptance that the work can't be done alone. It's easy for us to say we agree to this, but often when the conflict and disagreement arise we can quickly lose our appetite. The question is, how to not only surface the alternate views but stay with the 'heat' that then follows? There are a number of parts to this.

Firstly, this requires having a good awareness of what we represent in our role by our values, beliefs and ideologies. In other words, what faction might we represent in the system and in the world. If we are trying to resist taking sides or shutting down the alternate view, it's important to find a way to work as neutrally as possible, knowing that we can never completely abandon our views—nor is that useful. We can hold the conflict when we can show some distance at least temporarily from what and who we normally represent.

Secondly, that when the conflict arises it can be held. What helps here is to not frame what is being brought forward as personal. It is tempting to allow just one person or a predictable group to own the conflict and alternate views. This is convenient for everyone else. If it can be spread and shared among the group that's trying to work together, everyone can take a part in it. This will give relief and protection to the person raising the 'no', make it safe for other alternate views to surface, and loosen up the group to explore different roles and power patterns. Innovation cannot happen unless existing patterns of power change. It can be as simple as asking, 'Who else feels like this—even just a little bit?' At first, no-one may be willing to join the alternate view because bad things often happen to that view. In this case the role of authority may need to help it: 'Well, there's a little bit of me that feels like that... Let's explore it a bit more and see what we can learn from it.'

This will create a process that allows the wisdom that might be in the conflict to arise. For example, one group we worked with always started arguing about a particular business area when they were seeking to do something different. This stopped innovation and new conversations emerging. The person with authority found it hard to hold this conflict and as a result the conversations never seemed to go anywhere. When he was able to go deeper into the argument instead of seeing it as a diversion and an attack on him, the group was able to find some wisdom that allowed them to make progress. They found that their purpose was too unclear to do anything new and their ambitions were beyond their current competence. Until this conflict was held well by the authority role, the group wasted time cycling through the same arguments and the issues got personalised.

As this example implies, authority is often seen as the problem when the heat goes up. This is the last part of holding the 'no'. The role of authority can become a lightning rod for the frustrations and arguments that inevitably surface in any collaborative process for a range of reasons—they are seen to represent the status quo, are not quelling disagreement, are quelling disagreement too much, they might be getting things wrong, or people have had poor personal and systemic experiences with authority, to name just a few. When authority becomes the lightning rod, it is an indicator that the system has been disrupted and is having to start to learn new ways of working together. The expectations for people in authority to return everything back to normal are high; and when they don't deliver, it is inevitable that at one point or another that authority will get attacked. This usually has very little to do with what authority is doing or the person holding the role. But it can be difficult to bear and to hold from that role.

The task is to walk the fine line between getting completely deauthorised by the attack ('getting rolled') or snapping back at the attack and shutting down the alternate views. Holding steady in this middle place is one of the toughest challenges of the role of authority.

Not getting stuck in the 'no'

A holding environment needs to be 'tight at the edges and loose inside'. The loose part means that there's enough space for creativity, conflict and alternate voices to emerge and be worked with. The tight part is making sure the process of innovation can keep moving forward without getting too caught in the 'no'. This is the value of the holding environment. It helps groups to not get lost in the alternate views and derailed. The holding environment and purpose keep groups moving forward but with the wisdom that comes from the 'no' included.

However, consensus is not always possible. While there is wisdom in alternate views, it doesn't mean that all views can or will be implemented. In the desire to accommodate everyone or in the fear of disappointing, it is easy to become immobilised. After we have given room for all of the views to arise, we need a way to move forward. A decision needs to be made to implement something, leave something behind or take a specific route.

This is the point at which the role of authority needs to put forward a proposal and hear what is required for everyone to 'come along'. This isn't about whether the proposal should go ahead or not; it's about what people need if they're going to support it. This step is equally as important as giving space for the diversity of views to surface. Now that all the wisdom is available, the group needs to move forward with a workable solution that will inevitably not please everyone.

So what do people need to come along?

Interesting things happen at this juncture and with this question. Firstly, we are giving a clear signal that the group needs to move to another phase and that not everyone or every idea will be accommodated. Secondly, that those in authority show their interest in hearing what is required for people to support the proposal. This is different from trying to continue to lobby for an alternate proposal. The lobbying is over. Thirdly, requirements emerge that usually can be easy to accommodate and also give data on what some of the issues in implementing the proposal will be. And finally, it demonstrates that conflict is tolerable and still allow forward movement.

This is an important step in promoting innovation. In our work with groups we have found the experience of being able to hold conflict and bring the minority voice along to be very powerful. In one group of community leaders, the participants found it remarkable that they were able to go into the conflict, hear the 'no' voice, take onboard the requirements and still be able to continue working together. Their experience had been that groups often splintered at the point of conflict and therefore were unable to harness the wisdom of the 'no'.

Sometimes this question—What do people need to come along?—will generate responses that are impossible to accommodate: that there is nothing that can be done to get people to come along, no matter how much work went into creating the most open space for all the views to be heard. This happens particularly on deeply entrenched issues or with parties who have been in repeated dispute. When this occurs it signals there is much deeper conflict among the parties that often has little to do with the proposal in question. If this is the case, it is uncertain whether the innovation can be successfully implemented. That kind of conflict is beyond the bounds of the topic of innovation in this chapter. Nonetheless, if this stage is reached and not everyone will come along, we have still acquired very good information about what we may face in trying to implement our proposal—we will know who's in and who's out.

What's at stake

Conflict is easier to sell than do. It may not be for everyone—even in the form and purpose put forward here. It's important to recognise the potential losses here before talking about the hopes. It is hard to deal with the reality of breaking up the party. We may not be liked for a while or at least have to create situations where people are uncomfortable. If we carry a narrative of being liked and avoiding blame—that's going to be tough.

Hopefully this chapter has provided some skills and awareness on how to work with conflict to advance organisations and communities and why it is necessary. Because it is vital—even if we are scared of it and might not get it right—for our adaptation in Australia.

What are some of the things we may hope to innovate in Australia? Peace and prosperity for future generations? A sustainable way of living and population? Perhaps reconciliation between black and white Australia? A larger role in a changing world? These are big aspirations but they are not that different from the hopes we have for our more immediate environments—peaceful communities, resilient organisations, sustainable and prosperous lives, healing and harmony among us.

To achieve these hopes Australians need to foster innovation and model a new way of dealing with conflict. How we argue, not just how much we like each other, becomes critical.

> These arguments we have are a mark of our liberty. We can never forget that as we speak people in distant nations are risking their lives right now just for a chance to argue about the issues that matter.
>
> President Obama, Victory Speech, 2012

CHAPTER 13

DOING BUSINESS WITH AUTHORITY—THE WHY

Working upwards

Much has been written in the leadership literature about leading others. Yet it is rare to lead from the top of a system. The reality of leading is that we almost always need to work with people in authority positions that are 'above us' or influencing our work in ways that are out of our control. The CEO has to answer to a board, major customers and shareholders. The prime minister is beholden to voters, cabinet and minority parties. There is an illusion that moving to the top means one has more power. In fact, the higher up people go in a hierarchical sense, the more stakeholders need to be accommodated as there is more accountability and constraint. These constraints are typically unseen and unspoken. The same applies to informal power. The broader the reach and influence, the greater the expectation regarding this accountability.

This book has outlined how the Australian 'story' about authority influences the kind of relationship developed with those with more power and how that story influences the way the role of authority is taken up. It is crucial to maintain awareness of our automatic, knee-jerk type response to authority when we do not like its impact upon us, either personally and/or systemically. A lack of awarenes of these default reactions, risks two predictable responses: complying with or attacking authority. The easy way out is just to 'follow', which keeps the peace, at least in the short term, but doesn't provide what is required for successful interaction with authority. Followership relies on passivity in a way that is often not useful.

The more fashionable management idea about 'managing-up' in relationship with authority is an illusion. The idea that one can manage the boss ignores the reality of positional and social power and rank (see Chapter 10). By nature of their higher position in the hierarchy, those above cannot be managed by those below. They can be influenced, lobbied, kept in the dark, seductively enticed and even 'handled'—but not managed. The term managing-up is a misnomer that partly explains why it is hard to work well with senior authority roles. The idea that managing-up is an effective strategy for negotiating with those in senior positions is perpetuated because of a cultural preference to mask power and rank difference. A paradigm shift is required to work together across this difference.

To highlight this shift, in our work at Social Leadership Australia we use the phrase 'doing business with authority'. This way of thinking about the relationship recognises that both less and more senior roles have needs and potential benefits and costs in working together. It also highlights the need to recognise and work more effectively with the power differences.

As outlined earlier, authority is a resource that is needed to make progress. The phrase 'doing business' implies that while formal and informal authority is not balanced, there is something that both parties need from each other. This mutuality of need is typically confused for equality. While self-evident to some, naming this lack of equality is usually provocative in the Australian context. This is because power and rank difference is challenging to the Australian notion of equality. It can be interpreted as meaning that some people are better than others. What happens next is that there is a collusion either with that misunderstanding ('They are more important than me') or rebellion against it ('Who the hell do they think they are? No-one tells me what to do!'). Clearly, neither of these responses is useful and both get in the way of a productive way of doing business with authority.

There is a particular Australian dimension to this dynamic. All of the paradoxes in Australian leadership discussed in Part 2 centre on the role of authority and our relationship to it in ourselves and others. The Australian paradox of being simultaneously anti-authority and authority-dependent means that we are often unconscious about how we either comply with or rebel against authority. The transactional relationship with authority is complex, because of a simultaneous anti-authority public narrative *and* a subconscious desire to be cared for and nurtured by a more responsive and responsible authority. It is difficult to find a balanced relationship with authority and to see it as an important part of exercising leadership when we both don't want it but need its care.

> After years of consultation with the human services sector, a government department announces a new reform that aims to lead to positive outcomes for clients of the sector. The overall direction of the reform

is agreed on and the government department undertakes sector-wide engagement and consultation with the aim of co-creating the way services will operate on the ground. Firstly, the sector responds positively to the direction of the reform, then with mistrust. Questions start to emerge—'Is this genuine consultation?' 'Why don't they just tell us what they want to do?' 'Don't they know?' We already have the answers and things are working okay. The consultation process produces downloads of complaint rather than solutions.

In this example we see how the sector wants authority to have the answers and to tell them how to move forward. To accept that neither the government nor the sector has the answers may be almost inconceivable and unbearable. If no-one has the answers, both parties will be required to work together to come up with solutions. They will have to do business together.

It may seem obvious that we need to work with authority to make progress. But the role of authority mobilises people in different ways, but mostly into acts of either compliance or rebellion. A more nuanced place in between these polarities to intentionally work with and do business with authority is more difficult. Particularly in the beginning, it requires a sharpening of awareness and skills. It requires a new way of thinking and working with the role of authority.

Why bother working with authority?

Like it or not, making progress requires interaction with those who are higher up in the system and who have more power and rank. The focus here is doing business with people who have more systemic rank, or those with power that we don't have but need.

In considering how to do this, it is also useful to think about those who need to 'do business' with us in our role of authority;

There are five good reasons to do better business with authority:

Authority can't see everything

Authority has a limited view and is typically blind to new scenarios emerging in the system. It is easy for authority to have a blinkered and hence limited view of what's happening systemically. We know that the higher up we go, the less likely people are to tell us what is happening. Subordinates tend to be guarded about giving information to their seniors for fear of being micro-managed or looking bad. People in authority are not only blind to some of their subordinates' experience by virtue of being higher up in the system, they are inevitably further away from the frontline. This means that they are further away from the most up-to-date and usually the most important information about what is happening in the system.

> Several studies have shown that, 'Subordinates distort the information that they convey to their superiors, communicating upward in a way that minimises negative information, or withholds the information entirely . . . structuring groups into hierarchies automatically introduces restraints against free communication, particularly criticisms by low-status members toward those in higher-status positions.'[1]

Authority is vulnerable to distraction

People in authority are vulnerable to losing sight of the purpose of the work and their role. It is easy for them to be caught in side issues or brought down into 'the weeds' to solve other people's problems. The higher up the system we go, the more the focus needs to be on the 'why' and not the 'how' and the 'what'. Inevitably, there is a temptation and a seduction to be pulled into the fray—people like to be across what's going on and to be needed. Unfortunately, this distraction from purpose can be damaging to the role of authority or the system's progress. Usually both.

For example, during the first few years of a start-up consulting business, Mark focused on developing his team and their practice with clients, which was an important stage of the business's development. However, the processes the organisation used in their work with clients soon became the focal point of discussion and energy. Meanwhile, the team had become unclear on its purpose and direction and the organisation began floundering and became unsustainable.

Authority might be part of the problem

Authority is always indirectly part of the problem because it is not divorced from the system—it is the system's primary representative. This is the most benign form of being part of the problem. It can be much worse: authority can block progress, become corrupt or dangerous.

As a fairly new consultant within a consulting firm, Steve started to observe a culture of bullying. When he spoke to colleagues about it, he was told, 'That's just the way we get things done around here'. His direct manager was present when bullying took place and he would often join in with jokes about people. Steve wanted to raise the issue with his boss but wasn't sure whether his boss was colluding in it, doing something behind the scenes, or even saw it as a problem. Either way, he felt it was risky for him to engage his boss in the issue, as he may be targeted as the problem.

Authority is part of the holding environment

Authority is an important part of the holding environment in change and innovation. Permission is the simplest form of help but authority can offer a lot more than that—patronage, access to important stakeholders, sponsorship and resources to make the change.

As head of a government health department, Jo was aware of future policy directions that would have a significant impact on funding. She feared the impact this would have on the innovative work that her team was doing, which was starting to bear fruit. Jo explains, 'I needed to get the support from my bosses to ensure the work we had started would continue and at the same time protect my team from some of the uncertainty that was disrupting the department as a whole.' Since the start of the project Jo had kept her boss across all the developments in their initiative, feeding through outcomes as they emerged. At a time of crisis when funding cuts had just been announced and the government was facing a backlash, Jo's boss had a viable initiative to take to the ministerial level. The funding of Jo's work remained secure.

Authority as a resource

People in authority can offer valuable skills and insights; they have functional and political experience, skills and knowledge that can be of benefit.

Despite not feeling able to fully endorse and 'authorise' his CEO, Nick sought her out for advice about the development of a new idea. He was aware of his lack of knowledge on the subject and that his CEO had some experience that might be relevant. Nick not only found the information useful, but noticed how his CEO became animated when approached for advice. Nick guessed that she was aware of his difficulty in endorsing and authorising her and hoped that his search for guidance might further their potential partnership.

The challenge to systems to become more adaptive

Leadership facilitates organisations and communities to adapt to new realities. In order to do this we need to adapt our own practice: both how we use our authority and how we engage with those in authority. In an ideal world, when doing business well, partnering with authority utilises differences in rank for the benefit of the shared purpose and goals. If we are lucky, we will be met by authority figures that are interested in promoting systemic learning. But the reality is that even when they are interested in the systemic challenges facing the organisation, they may not be in a position to resource the change because of multiple other competing commitments and constraints. In a state of overwhelm, people in authority may react with cynicism or disinterest. At worst they may react with an offensive or at least defensive reaction because the actions of those below have been perceived as a threat.

Change generated from below can be difficult. Managers may profess to want those below to exercise leadership, but it can be threatening when it actually happens. From the position of authority, the mere suggestion of change may seem like a threat as it implies that the system for which they are responsible is not working.

This is the inevitable downside of taking up the role and functions of authority. One of these functions is that of protecting the system and its individual members. The negative side of protecting the system and its members is that any criticism or suggestion of change can be interpreted as a threat—despite good intentions and a desire to remain open to adaptive suggestions. There is a part of this that is an ego-reaction to being criticised (directly or indirectly) but there is also a part that instinctively protects the system for which one is responsible. Social Leadership Australia (SLA) regularly facilitates dialogue between different organisational levels, particularly between CEOs and executive teams and the level below them. Almost universally, a critique from the level below generates defensiveness in the level above. This is a natural human tendency.

The fruit vendor in Tunisia who sparked the Arab Spring uprisings across the Middle East and the middle manager in a corporation who feels she can't speak the truth to her boss have something in common. Both feel that they are limited in their options when dealing with authority. This is a global tendency. So most rely on their ability to feign compliance, or muster an attack or a rebellion against authority (overt or covert). There are other options. But what are they and gets in the way of seeing them?

Before exploring these questions it is important to be mindful of the environment. In North Korea or Burma, the ability to speak to and challenge authority is lower than it is in Australia. This does not mean that it is impossible to speak to and challenge authority, but it does mean that the skills and practices described in the coming pages require a scrutiny and awareness about authority's ability to deal with being challenged and the personal risks that are likely involved.

The goal is to find more creative options for working with authority. To begin, why is it that Australians in particular think that compliance, rebellion, enticement or attack are the only options? If authority can't be avoided, there is an opportunity to find a way to productively engage with it. Ronald Heifetz calls this trying to exercise leadership from the 'foot of the table'.[2] There are useful techniques to do this, but first we need to take an honest look at our own story about authority as herein lies the biggest challenge.

Our stories about authority

The challenge to find a useful personal and systemic way of working with authority begins as teenagers (if not earlier) and resurfaces throughout life. Sometimes we deal with it much like how we did back then. This area of personal growth and development is not only an individual learning edge—it also belongs to the world's learning and development. It begins with understanding what influences how we interact with authority—or how we are mobilised towards it.

The world story

Finding a way to better work with those in authority is a world challenge. The role of authority is a big archetypal role—one that transgresses culture, age and time. Like many other archetypes (e.g. mother, father, doctor, victim and tyrant), it carries lots of projections formed over the period of human history.

This history has generated many stories about authority that are generally wrapped up in myth and biography about those qualities and figures that are commonly call 'leaders'. From Nelson Mandela to Mother Theresa, Martin Luther King and John Frances Kennedy, they are mostly male and are often characterised by militaristic-type accessories and heroic journeys. This world story about leadership is mostly concerned with overcoming adversity because this is the archetypal path of the hero (and occasional heroine). There seems to be little distinction made between good and poor outcomes, or good and bad values. Hitler, Genghis Khan and Mao Tse Tung are generally cited as examples of leaders—not specifically 'good ones' or 'good ones with bad outcomes', just leaders. This limits the narrative, not only about leaders but also about authority. It reflects the story of human growth, survival and conquest without much qualification or evaluation. It also presents a challenge for the contemporary relationship to authority. What role does authority play in the contemporary context characterised by an annual reduction in the level of global conquest and war, and populations of people who are increasingly becoming more educated and connected?

Despite a global increase in peace and prosperity, the world has not yet found a way to engage with the role of authority in a way that facilitates human development. High expectations are often quickly followed by bitter disappointment. When all else fails authority is removed by whatever means possible—the ballot box, exile or assassination. The world story of authority perpetuates a cycle of heroes and fans followed by tyrants and victims.

The universal story

The narrative about authority also has an 'out of world' dimension. Most human systems identify a higher level of authority that is in some form above the human species. Many cultures project their authority onto gods and supernatural belief as an omnipresent and omniscient way of being in relationship with authority.

Whether we call this being God, Allah, Buddha, or designate some other central figure or force as the ultimate authority, the role is characterised by universally agreed functions and qualities—whether these be judge and judgement, life and nurture, enlightenment, growth or punishment.

The context story

Particularly in Western countries, there is a desire to be told what to do while being ambivalent or rejecting the notion that someone else can be 'above'. We have discussed the manifestation of this notion in the paradoxes of leadership and authority in Australia in Part 2.

Like many nation states the Australian narrative about authority is informed by history. However, unlike many others, Australia is a relatively young nation and still flexible enough to potentially see this transformed. Australians in authority cannot discount the impact of history and how this constructs the way that we react to and take up the role of authority.

Being an Australian and being among Australians has an impact. The strength and effect of this impact is difficult to comprehend due to our relative isolation and the fact we are mostly doing business with ourselves. It provides a specific cultural context on how authority is viewed and this view impacts and structures how Australians relate to those with higher rank. This cultural lens can be a source of freedom or bondage. The paradox of being anti-authority and authority-dependent can be an obstacle in doing business with authority, but it is not set in stone.

The system story

The experience of authority begins in family life and then broadens to other larger systems and institutions, in particular school and early jobs. The importance of these early experiences has been the subject of much research. More recently, in the employment domain, terminology such as 'career imprinting' has been developed to highlight the role that early experiences play in the view of work throughout a career.

For example, Liz's experience of authority at school was one of feeling punished for breaching rules that were inconsistently applied. Her relationship to authority in the workplace began with mistrust and cynicism until experience proved otherwise. This led her to seek out management roles in more collaborative environments.

The personal story

Of course, there is a personal element to the history and experience of authority. Have we been met with optimism, respect, interest and support? When have we been de-authorised, ignored, attacked or scapegoated? Have we been made to feel empowered or disempowered by authority? Do we walk around with a basic trust, or are we ambivalent about or strongly mistrustful of authority? Do we begin with cynicism, hope or fear? These things affect the automatic responses to and default positions towards authority.

Facing things as they are

From the universal through to the personal, the response to authority has been constructed by these life experiences. This reaction is often beyond most people's awareness or control. The first step in trying to better do business with authority involves bringing awareness to this. It also gives us clues as to how we might be likely to act in the role of authority ourselves and allows a better use of rank when relating 'downwards'. In this process of rewriting the narrative is an opportunity to develop more compassion for the blocks that other people likely experience in dealing with us.

There can be good reason for having real trouble when working with authority. As outlined in the paradox chapters, sometimes authority can be intentionally abusive or neglectful. Even with good intentions it is important to accept that:

- Authority is flawed—There is no way that the role of authority can be taken up in a way that will please everyone. In exercising leadership this imperfection is heightened because change inevitably incurs loss. Personal loss is usually keenly felt.
- Authority figures are human—It is often hard to accept that those who occupy the role of authority are human beings and susceptible to mistakes. They have biases and, while they might have some answers, they don't have them all. It is difficult to both disappoint and to be disappointed. This can turn into an expectation of perfection both from those below and from authority onto itself.
- Authority is mostly transient—It is something that exists rather than something that can be owned.

In many ways authority is a role for which the script was written long ago and edited over time by culture and context.

With awareness of the different stories of authority and their origin, we can begin to think and act differently in doing business with the role.

CHAPTER 14

DOING BUSINESS DIFFERENTLY— THE HOW

The role of authority is crucial to the practice of better leadership. Authority carries many projections and expectations. To make progress requires working with those with more authority, power and rank. This is what we are calling doing business with authority. Doing better business with authority requires a transformation in ourselves and our context. It is a systemic challenge in itself. The following section sets out what is required to adapt and become more effective in doing business with authority. This section is organised in two parts: the first focuses on doing the groundwork and the second looks at utilising different skills and techniques.

The groundwork

There are a number of things that can be done to increase awareness of what leaders typically face in the role of authority and how we typically respond to the role. This groundwork is needed before bringing any particular 'business' to authority.

Awareness of our story and yearnings

As discussed earlier, there are many stories that impact the relationship with authority and expectations of the role. Before we do business with authority, we need to be aware of how our stories impact our expectations and structure how we take up an authority role, as well as how we relate to the role. The worksheet at the end of this chapter is designed to increase awareness in these areas.

The view from above

Authority has a broader view of the world and more power to connect to its diverse constituents. What is often not seen is that while people in authority have this potential, they are beholden to those constituents. They can see more from their higher position, but often can do less. It is important to understand the needs and constraints upon authority at any given moment. For example, authority is typically under pressure from particular factions or constituents. They similarly struggle with authority figures in more senior positions higher up in the system. Who are they beholden to and what do those constituencies need?

Timing and capacity

Systems are typically in flux and as a result the pressures on authority are often changeable. This pressure becomes more constant the higher the authority role. The capacity of authority to hear, understand and take on a request from below changes from moment to moment. This may sound obvious, but it is often overlooked because we view the role for its potential rather than see its constraint. Timing is crucial.

A senior police officer tells the story about having an unpopular and difficult policy waiting in a desk drawer for many years. The need for the policy is taken more seriously after a triggering incident creates enough heat for the policy to be tabled. In the context of this heat, the police commissioner is grateful to receive it. Despite having dismissed it on several previous occasions, the commissioner announced the introduction of the policy at the next press conference.

Authority is always facing pressure that will convince those in the role that there is never a good time to make a change. One executive who we worked with had a practice of letting their authority figure know that they had something to address by beginning with, 'I need to work with you on X and I'm wondering when it would be good to bring that to you.' This flags the intention while checking how interested authority is in the idea without demand or obligation on either side.

Unmet demands or realistic progress

It is easy to mistake meetings as a forum to conclude a piece of business rather than a step in making progress in negotiating business. In our SLA consultancy work with managers, we frequently encounter the expectation that the outcome which people want will be gained as a result of one meeting. This sounds like everyone is crystal clear about what we want and when we want it. On the contrary, we are often unclear on our exact purpose and fail to identify or communicate what we are looking for from authority. Is it a sign-off or permission? Is our purpose to keep them up to date? Or extract a decision? Do we want their benign involvement?

One of Geoff's earlier managers identified that he was often unclear on what he expected from her and would help him out by asking: 'So what is it you are looking for me to do on this today?' Over time Geoff began to prepare in advance and think about what he was actually looking for in each interaction. He came to routinely identify whether what he wanted was realistic or whether his goals could be best met as part of a plan over time. Any interaction with authority consumes one of their most valuable resources—time.

Understanding . . . reputation

Fortunately or not, everyone carries a reputation in the systems in which they work. Some help and some get in the way. These reputations are also in flux depending on recent achievements. Word gets around. This impacts the willingness and interest of authority to engage with us, and how this potential interest will be perceived by other constituents in the system. Considering and understanding our long-term and recent reputation prepares us to gauge how interested and willing people in authority will be to work with us and what we may need to do to prepare. For example, if we find out that we are seen as always raising the problems in the system, we may need to show a different side of ourselves to avoid becoming predictable. Becoming stuck in any one particular role makes us vulnerable to being 'scapegoated'. In any case it is worth considering the impact of our reputation on the reputation of authority. Does doing business with you help or hinder the reputation of authority in the broader system?

Understanding and owning our power and rank

Reputation is a form of power in working with authority. As discussed in Chapter 10 power and rank can attract and hold the attention of authority. This is often underestimated. It is drawn from several sources including personal power, from experience and reputation, as well as social and psychological rank. It is also factional. Factional rank comes from those with whom we are seen to be aligned—functionally, ideologically, geographically and historically. This factional power, like personal power, goes up and down depending on what is happening around and in the system. Knowing about these sources of power will provide a gauge of how interested or compelled those in authority might be in negotiating with us. It may mean a stronger power base is required to get attention from authority.

Owning the mess

In holding a role of authority, being the receptacle of other people's problems and complaints is tiring. As is the expectation that authority will fix everything, partially because such complaints can feel like an attack on the system for which authority is responsible. Rarely do those bringing the complaint also bring insight into how they are contributing to the problem. Without this insight, strategies for change are limited. Thinking this through in a way that positions us as part of the problem facilitates some spaciousness in the transaction. This can transform a problem from one that is projected onto the level above to one that is to be solved together.

Skills and techniques

Doing the necessary groundwork provides the awareness to engage more usefully with authority. But there are also skills and techniques which can facilitate progress.

Meta-communicating

Creativity and innovation emerge from diversity and the ability of an organisation to work through conflict, between different levels of power. Despite the best preparation and intention, differences in power, perspective, needs and desires inevitably mean that the relationship between organisational levels in the hierarchy can get stuck. This is especially disadvantageous when 'stuckness' perseveres. It doesn't go away, it goes underground.

Instead of increasing the stuckness or creating unnecessary conflict with authority, we can try to get on the balcony. The skill of meta-communicating is being able to communicate the dilemma from the balcony and not just the dance floor.

There are some practical steps required in moving between the floor and the balcony:

- Step one involves noticing negative feedback. Everyone can argue the case for what they think will work—if only everyone else could get it! In this type of scenario we need to notice that everyone else or at least many others are giving negative feedback to our idea. If there is positive feedback to our idea, we do not need to argue.
- Step two requires us to stop advocating for our idea and switch to explaining what the challenge is like from our role or position. How we do this is as important as the message itself. We are endeavouring to neutrally communicate about the difficulty in the communication. For example, 'I'm a bit stuck on this issue. I feel it is important for our organisation, but can't seem to make any progress. I'm wondering if there's something I'm doing or not doing that is not helping or perhaps I don't understand enough about your perspective?' Questions like this provide a shortcut to the heated back-and-forth volley between different 'sides' of an issue and invite all the sides to refocus on it as a shared problem. This is based on the knowledge that all parts of a system are crucial to its functioning.

Meta-communication can be quite simple: 'I'm feeling frustrated on how to make progress on this. Can you give me some advice on what you would do if you were me?' This won't always work but it usually gives a good perspective on what else may be happening that you might have missed. Demonstrating a willingness to see oneself as part of the problem is relieving, particularly when working with authority.

Seeking to minimise loss

Surprisingly there is often an expectation that those in authority will help implement a proposal and little thought is given to what losses they may incur in backing them. In times of change there is always some kind of loss. Backing one thing often means a loss of something else. It could be a tangible loss, like redirecting the budget from one area to another, or a loss of face and reputation. Backing a proposal could hurt authority's standing with another important faction in the system. Indeed, the loss could be for authority itself.

There is often little understanding or exploration of this potential loss. Even if there is some awareness of it, there is little interest provided by the level below in trying to support the transition and mitigate the loss. Working with authority to map out how losses can be minimised for them and others is crucial. We are also more likely to get 'repeat business' with this authority figure whether or not they appreciate the systemic lens that we are able to bring.

Doing more than asking

Watching *Q&A* on ABC television or listening to any public engagement with a politician, we see how skilled and relentless we are at asking (and expecting) authority in Australia to do something for us. This one-way traffic is often explained with the phrase, 'That's why you get paid the big bucks!' It can be exhausting to be treated as someone else's ATM. Our experience in the role of authority and with others with whom we work shows how rarely people in authority are asked what they need—and how their functions can be supported. In trying to do business with authority this is a useful consideration. What might authority figures need to be able to fulfil our demands, but more generally the demands of the system?

Modelling boundaries

By nature of the hierarchy, the level above is always more generalist than the level below. So while authority relies on the level below for frontline data and knowledge of particular functions, stakeholders or issues, it does not have the freedom to completely back specific proposals. At the level below, the downside of representing one view or faction is that they can be seen as evangelists for a narrow cause.

To avoid the risk of being seen as an evangelist (and becoming predictable) it is useful to consider carefully how our role or interest help meet a broader organisational purpose. How does our role or view link with the other parts of the system? It demonstrates that we can see the bigger picture as well as our part in it from the perspectives of both the balcony and dance floor.

Appreciation and compassion

In the paradox of both rejecting authority yet needing it, frustrations are easily projected onto authority. When authority figures let us down, or don't do what we want them to do, the perceived breach of trust can be immobilising or mobilises us to go into combat. Systems with a perceived 'failure' by authority can easily revert back to default responses of complaint and attack, despite any trust that may have already been established. A way through this cycle can be to identify and reflect on our own authority and see this 'failure' in ourselves. This exercises compassion for the person in the role and the progress they are trying to make, as well as toward ourselves—because ultimately we know that we, too, can be in that role and also fail others' expectations.

Those in authority very rarely get positive feedback from their systems. They will know when people in the system are unhappy but there can be a deathly silence when things are going well. This is not only challenging for those in authority but it is also dangerous for the system. When people in authority don't have any benchmarks on what they are doing well or where progress is being made other than themselves, they will often miss important data on the strengths that they and their system need to build on. They need to know what to keep on doing, as well as what not to do. We all need affirmation, to know that something we are doing is working.

Traps

Doing business with authority is always tricky. Sometimes there is success and sometimes there is failure. There are a number of traps:

- **Thinking we are equal**—It is easy to confuse equality as humans for equality of rank. Those higher in the hierarchy do not have equal power; they have more. Indeed, in our work at Social Leadership Australia we have seen our own confusion in this issue. We used to call this whole skill area of doing business with authority 'partnering with authority'. We found that the idea of partnering with authority was confusing for

leaders as it implied equality: it didn't recognise the reality of dealing with differences in rank.
- **Becoming the lightning rod**—If we fail to understand the constraints that those in authority are under, it is very easy for us to become the problem. Given the role of authority is primarily to maintain the status quo of our systems, drawing attention to issues or problems can be interpreted as a threat. The more we become fixed in the role of the person who is always dissenting or complaining, the more of a threat we can become. The voice of dissent is really important in any system, but what's more important is knowing how to occupy that role well. When we don't, others can use us to be their spokesperson, to take all the risks by voicing their concerns.
- **Getting enticed or 'seduced' by authority**—It is easy to get enticed or 'seduced' by authority; often this is without any conscious intent from either side. Those trying to make change with good motivation and intelligence can find themselves enticed into a more benign relationship with authority. It is easy to be 'favoured into silence'. This can be exacerbated as one's formal authority grows because all of a sudden there is more to lose in challenging the status quo. Holding on to purpose can be difficult but is a good antidote to enticement and seduction. 'What am I supposed to achieve in this role—is what's going on now in service of that purpose?' or 'Am I serving my own interests and keeping authority happy?' Useful questions to ask.
- **Reverting to attack or compliance**—In the challenge of working with authority it is easy to revert to well-worn pathways or default positions. For most this will likely involve one of two options: to comply, or to rebel and attack. This is a common pattern that is well supported by Australia's culture.

Once again, most of the work is first of all having an awareness about our pattern and being able to ask ourselves if our response is useful. By holding steady to the central purpose of our organisation or community and being clear on role, we are freer to work with a more diverse range of options.

- **Authority as a teacher**—There is an old adage that we get the leaders we deserve. Given the word 'leader' usually means authority figure, perhaps we get the authority figures we deserve. This adage is usually interpreted exclusively in the negative. It implies that leadership can be used as a type of punishment for who we are or how we are acting. A more useful interpretation might be that the authority figures we do business with are there for a reason. What if, together, we are learning to transform the exercise of leadership and our response to that? We may well get the authority figures that we deserve so we can learn from them.

Ultimately how we do business with authority is an illustration of the relationship that we have with our own inner authority and how we do business with ourselves. The more uncomfortable and dismissive we are with authority figures, the bigger the barrier for us in fulfilling the functions of authority ourselves. Authority is an important resource for progressing institutions and communities. Learning to own, appreciate and develop the skills and awareness to use authority well presents a significant opportunity to make real change and have a positive social impact.

Worksheets

The purpose of these activities is to bring awareness to the challenges and opportunities that we face in doing business with authority.

Exercise 1: Your story with authority

Family
- What was the authority structure in your family?
- How well did the authority in your family provide direction, protection and order?
- What were the traditional roles in the family and who made the decisions?
- What stories have you learnt about authority from your ancestors?

Institutions
- How was authority exercised at school?
- How did you respond?
- What was your experience of authority in your first work institution?
- How did you respond?

Cultural context
- What are the stories about authority from your country or culture?
- How do they impact on your response to authority?

Looking at your responses to the questions above, how would you describe your current relationship with authority?

Exercise 2: A current challenge

1. Think about a particular authority figure that is currently challenging. How is your story with authority playing out in this situation?

2. What do you need to be more aware of to make progress in doing business with authority?

   - Authority's view of the world
   - Pace and capacity of authority
   - Your reputation, authority's and the system's
   - Understanding and owning your power and rank
   - What's your piece of the mess?

3. What skills would be useful to help make progress in doing business with authority?

CHAPTER 15

MORE THAN SURVIVING

Resilience is about facing adversity with hope.[1]

ANNE DEVESON

Being

There are things we need to *know* and *do* to have a positive impact in leadership. These can all be learned. The preceding chapters have explored those that we believe are the most important, particularly in the Australian context. The final, and equally important, aspect of leadership is also the most amorphous. It is the 'being' of leadership.[2]

It has been left to the last chapter as it is often the first and most common mistake to be made about leadership. Namely, that leadership is solely about who we are and not what we do: that leaders are born and not made. This chapter challenges the idea that there are inherent qualities which permit some to lead.

The *being* of leadership is the acceptance of strengths and gifts as well as flaws and vulnerabilities. In other words, it is finding a way to lead that is congruent with who we are. Finding a congruous way of being (and leading) has a number of advantages. Firstly, it is important in how we *know* and *do* leadership. For example, as discussed in Chapter 11, to be useful in roles of authority requires a good understanding of what unique sources of power we bring to a role. Secondly, and the focus of this chapter, is that if we aim to lead in a way that is both personally sustainable and inspires others to want to lead as well, then how we *are* in that role is as important as what we do.

It is easy to lose perspective, purpose and hope in the face of the often hard realities of exercising leadership. Skill, good intentions and strong motivation do not prevent attack, denial, blame or scapegoating. Moreover, the assets and strengths we bring can understandably encourage a system to abdicate the hard work—we are often happy to allow someone else to make the effort.

Leadership often requires not only supporting a system through its losses but also enduring personal loss. This can be the loss of credibility, status, power, resources and certainty that change brings about. It applies equally to a system as it does to those personally exercising leadership.

In the face of loss, scrutiny and the weight of expectations, many ask themselves whether the cost is too high. It is easy to become overworked, stressed, burned out or pushed out. It's not a very enticing picture for anyone thinking about having a positive impact. More commonly, people lose the qualities of heart that led them to yearn to lead in the first place. After all, it is impossible to meet everyone's expectations—perhaps especially our own.

Enduring this kind of difficulty is often called resilience. Unfortunately, this word can imply a quality of enduring and surviving that is also less than inspiring. It often doesn't inspire others to want to join the work. Is there an alternative? Is there a way of working that is sustainable for individuals and systems, one that models a way of leading that is enticing to others? Is it possible to lead and bring all of who we are to the work of creating positive change?

Leadership needs to mean more than surviving. If it is an important part of how we live as humans then, like humanity, it is not just about survival but also growth, joy and togetherness. This requires a different way of thinking about *being* in leadership. And thankfully, like knowing and doing, it can also be learned.

Reflections on surviving and thriving

Stephanie has been a CEO in the NGO sector for nearly twenty years. She has managed several community-based organisations working with disadvantaged groups:

> I've always had a lot of freedom to create the environments I want to work in. Once I get to know people I'm warts and all and have tended to not keep too much back for myself.
>
> This has attracted me to the energy of organisations that are growing and developing. I love the creativity, energy and the buzz of getting a new organisation or approach off the ground. So, as my current workplace has developed, it was easy to stay in the norm of trying new things and being creative. Meanwhile, more day-to-day, operational areas needed to be maintained and developed. Over a period of time I found I had taken on more operational work while still being keen to develop new initiatives. I wasn't very good at letting go of things. There was a systemic pull; the more I said yes, the more the organisation got increasingly reliant on me being able to do the work. When I got to a place where I was saying, 'I can't do this any more', it

was very hard to get others to pay attention to this because at the same time I was saying yes to all the new exciting developments.

I was struggling to cope. I wanted to maintain the level and position I'd worked hard for *and* take on new things. People often comment on how strong and capable I am. While part of that is true, there's a collusion in it. The organisation was allowing me to be a buffer and there was no buffer for me. Strong doesn't mean invincible.

Unfortunately, the more I got overwhelmed, the more rigid I became. I found minor setbacks hard to cope with and started to get into a lot of conflict. The work started to feel heavy and it stopped being creative and fun. I felt I was used up and had lost my compassion. I ended up burning out.

It feels very different now. I show up differently. I'm clearer about boundaries, I don't bring in all of me any more. By focusing on why I'm there and the requirements of the role, I'm able to more easily identify whether what I'm doing is useful for the organisation and me. The main learning for me has been about letting go. Letting go of this idea that we will always get it right and the disappointment that comes when we don't. I have had to let go of the idea that I need to be involved in everything or can do everything. I have to catch myself by being clear on whether my role needs me to get involved. Most of all, I feel like I can now bring a lightness to my work and ironically, by having more boundaries in place, I can bring more of who I am to my role.

Andrew is a partner in a management consulting firm. His organisation has gone through significant change over a number of years. He describes how he had to learn to fulfil his authority role:

My main challenge in leadership has been working out what's required in my role. When I came into this role I knew it required a different approach to what had gone before but wasn't sure how to bring myself into it.

There have been times when this role has been very difficult. For the first time in my life I have had a CEO who wasn't supportive and simultaneously we were under significant financial pressure. I felt that the people around me didn't have the skill to handle this new environment and it impacted on my relationship with them.

I realised that I could swing from being very personal and open, to hardening up and being quite mistrustful. It's a bit of a default that I end up going it alone when I don't know who I can trust. Of course it had the impact that the team questioned their trust in me. It wasn't very useful and became a vicious cycle. I became quite compartmentalised, engaging with people purely around their role, and it was a hard place to be as I censored a lot of how I was feeling about what was going on. The team wasn't able to see where I was struggling and I didn't feel able to ask for help.

Being clearer on what I'm trying to do and being able to let people know the impact of what's going on has helped me find a middle ground. I've been clearer on what's needed from my role and let people support me. I have also been able to be clearer on where they need to improve and that I won't just step in and fix things for them.

Larissa Behrendt is a university professor and a national commentator and advocate on Indigenous issues:

I have found that being strategic about what you spend your energy on makes you much better. That was the light bulb moment for me—knowing that if I said no to the things I didn't really want to do, I would do the things I wanted to do so much better because I had more time and energy for them. Saying no is a hard thing to do, particularly as a privileged woman from a culture where reciprocity is more important.

So what's important is for me to find a way to appreciate what my strengths are in a way that stops me from being flattered or cajoled into something I'm not good at, or to be someone I'm not. It allows me to think about how I use what I'm good at to do the things I think are important—to think about what is it with the role I'm in that means I can have practical outcomes, rather than what is it with the role that gives me status. I see it as a trap for a lot of younger Indigenous people coming through. They are talented and clever but they get seduced. There's a whole generation of very bright young Indigenous people. I've seen them get caught up with their own press and it ends up that you don't hear from them for a few years because they've lost their way.

You have to be really thick-skinned. The nature of the work I do makes me incredibly unpopular in lots of places, but I think the work is really important so it's worth doing; you get less precious about it and don't waste energy on the places you can't get movement.

Creating the space in your life that's your private space where you can be away from work, where you're nurtured, have a loving family, supportive partner and other things you're doing out of the work context is important. I haven't always had the balance right. You have to create parts of your life where you can find strength, otherwise you can't do the other stuff.

Letting go

These stories have recurring themes. The first is that those in positions of authority trying to exercise leadership can end up becoming caricatures. It is easy to become a caricature of the hard worker, the super-competitive, the one everyone loves or the all-knowing. These caricatures can bend people out of shape and they end up behaving in ways that are not useful or sustainable for themselves or their systems. We can end up being overworked and losing our way. The lure of these caricatures is powerful.

The second theme is that to escape the caricature and lead in a way that is more than just surviving requires letting go of the traditional ideas about what leadership requires. It is often counterintuitive:

- When we let go of control and acknowledge the power we have, we are able to value others and work across difference.
- When we are clear on our purpose, we can let go of the exhausting effort of trying to maintain control.
- When we are aware of our power and use it well, we can be more compassionate and less authoritarian.
- When we are clear on our role, we are able to use it as a boundary and anchor to navigate us through the confusion of change.
- When we can promote and tolerate conflict well, relationships and systems can become stronger and more innovative.
- When we are better able to work with roles of authority, we can have more freedom and power, not less.

It is our capacity to step into the unknown with others that allows us to bring our better selves to the work of leadership. To do this we need to trust ourselves, step off the solid ground of what we know, to be present and open to what emerges. This way of being can be counterintuitive when our conditioning is to stay safe and hold on to what we know. Liz recalls the similarities between this cusp of leadership and being in deep water:

I grew up scared of going in the water. In the shallow end, I can keep myself afloat and can relax and let go when I know I can touch the bottom. Then I really enjoy being in the water. As soon as I go out of my depth I start to panic and hold on even more tightly to whoever is around me. I know in those moments what I need to do is breathe, let go and trust myself and the people around me to help me stay afloat and be there in case I go under. My senses scream in the opposite direction but when I let go I float.

This kind of letting go allows us to go to the deep end of leadership and not drown. It also allows others to join us because 'We might understand that one day others may think of us and see it is possible to do hard work and have a light life.'[3] We may see there is the possibility to lead and have a joyful life. This might be how we can bring the distinctive part of being Australian—our openness, lightness and relaxed nature—to what is otherwise a heavy idea of leadership in the world.

If we can lead in this way, not only can we do more than survive, we might find that soon we are not alone. It will look like a good path to be on.

CHAPTER 16

A NEW AUSTRALIAN LEADERSHIP STORY

The old story

For many years Australians have been uneasy with power. We have complained about it and avoided it in ourselves and others. We wanted it but were scared of it, having seen what it did when it failed. We have looked to others both overseas and 'higher up' for the answers. These have been confusing times when it has been easy to be seduced by false visions, negativity, fear and individual obsession. We struggle at times to understand who we are and what we really care about. There are many resources and good intentions, but we have lacked the skill to avoid the traps of those who went before.

A new story

Australia has an opportunity to write a new story about leadership. This story is one that engages all Australians and offers a chance to do what our national anthem captures so succinctly in its title: to *Advance Australia Fair*. This title goes to the core of what leadership is all about—making progress together and for each other. It is an expression of what is already valued and prized in Australian life even though it may not yet be bound to the practice and conception of leadership.

Leadership is always about trying to solve our own problems, making progress and leaving things better than we found them. This is an idea of leadership that is more than just one-dimensional. It brings together the social, economic, cultural and environmental needs of society.

Australians are practical and action-oriented people. This is fortunate because leadership and adaptation lies in the *doing*: the constant striving, effort, recalibrating and learning. It is more than a hope and desire for things to be better, it is a constant and unending process and relationship with one another. It is a process of transformation that never ends.

For Australians, this opportunity for transformation lies in the shadows of the paradoxes of Australian leadership. Here we can find the seeds of our future development:

- Our cynicism can be transformed into a willingness to face how things are. This brings practicality to the work of leadership.
- Our complaint can be transformed into energy for our own action, engagement and authorisation. This brings power to the work of leadership.
- Our disillusionment can be transformed into a curiosity for new solutions. This brings innovation to the challenges we face.
- Our ambivalence for power can be reconciled with accepting and valuing power. This brings compassion and wisdom to the people we lead.

- Our uneasiness with conflict can be overcome by the value we place on real relationships. This brings optimism to dealing with difference and diversity

These transformations inevitably mean much more than writing a new leadership story. They are part of being human. As humans we are not willing to just accept how things are. We don't just accept how power is held, who holds it, how it is used and for what purpose. We don't just struggle for power and dominance as humans, we also struggle to do something useful with it. We are compelled to move forward and to make progress. And we struggle to do that at the same as caring for each other.

We care about leadership because we can't help ourselves. It's part of being human. We cannot resist the desire to make progress and improve things, no matter how many times we and others have failed. The work can be daunting and often we may hope that others would take up this role. But if we have some power and want to use it well, we can make a contribution. This is a human story as well as a leadership story.

In Australia we are in this position now. We have enough room to do something useful, not just for Australia but further afield. When we begin to share responsibility for our fate and are brave enough to trust ourselves to experiment and fail, we can overcome the biggest hurdle—being brave enough to think we can succeed.

This story is something that is still possible in Australia, perhaps more possible than anywhere else. To quote the Australian Productivity Commissioner, Robert Fitzgerald, this kind of understanding and practice is still achievable 'because Australia is still a relatively small nation, it is still relatively uncomplicated'. In other words, we still have room to move.

With this room to move we have an opportunity to experiment in writing a new story about leadership. We share this task.

This venture we call Australia was always an experiment. It has taken us a long time to see it in this light, and even longer to accept the lightness, the freedom, the possibility that offers in a way of being. It keeps us on our toes, as curious observers of ourself. It has made us value quick reflexes and improvisation—lightness in that sense too. It ought to make us skeptical of conclusions, of any belief that where we are now is more than a moment along the way. An experiment is open, all conclusions provisional. Even the conclusiveness of a full stop is no more, so long as there is breath, than a conventional gesture towards pause in a continuing argument.

David Malouf[1]

ENDNOTES

Introduction

1. The Australian Hansard, Parliament of Australia, July 6, 2011.
2. Horne, D., *The Lucky Country*, Penguin Publishing, Melbourne, 2009.
3. Soueif, A., *The Guardian*, London, March 8, 2011.
4. Clark, M., *A Short History of Australia*, Penguin Publishing, Melbourne, 1995.

Chapter 1

1. Megalogenis, G., 'Trivial Pursuit: Leadership and the end of the reform era', *Quarterly Essay 40*, Black Ink Books, Melbourne, 2010.
2. *ABC Mornings with Jon Faine*, 774 ABC Melbourne, Australian Broadcasting Corporation
3. Pew Research Centre's Project for Excellence in Journalism, 2011.
4. Civics Expert Group, *Whereas the people: Civics and citizenship education*, Australian Government Publication Services, Canberra, 1994.

5 Brett, J., & Moran, A., *Ordinary People's Politics*, Pluto Press, Melbourne, 2006.
6 Watson, D., *Recollections of a Bleeding Heart—A portrait of Paul Keating PM*, Vintage Books, Sydney, 2011.
7 Heifetz, R., *Leadership Without Easy Answers*, Harvard University Press, 1994.
8 Newton, J., Long,S. & Sievers, B., *Coaching in Depth: The organizational role analysis approach*, Karnac, London, 2005.
9 Horne, D., *The Lucky Country*, Penguin Publishing, Melbourne, 2009.
10 Wikipedia entry on *The Wizard of Oz* film, http://en.wikipedia.org/wiki/The_Wizard_of_Oz_(1939_film).

Chapter 2

1 Watson, D., *Recollections of a Bleeding Heart—A portrait of Paul Keating PM*, Vintage Books, Sydney, 2011.
2 Heifetz, R., *Leadership Without Easy Answers*, Harvard University Press, Cambridge, 1994.
3 Aigner, G., *Leadership Beyond Good Intentions*, Allen & Unwin, Sydney, 2011.
4 Heifetz, R. & Linsky, M., *Leadership on the Line: Staying alive through the dangers of leading*, Harvard Business School Press, Boston, 2002.

Chapter 3

1 Aigner, G., *Leadership Beyond Good Intentions*, Allen & Unwin, Sydney, 2011.

Chapter 4

1 Kelly, P., *The End of Certainty*, Allen & Unwin, Sydney, 2008.
2 Tingle, L., 'Great Expectations: Government, entitlement and an angry nation', *Quarterly Essay 46*, Black Ink Books, Melbourne, 2012.

REFERENCES

3 Roy Morgan Reserarch, Australia's Constitutional Future: Opinion Polling, Presented to Australians for Constitutional Monarchy, October 8, 2011.
4 Malouf, D., 'Made in England: Australia's British inheritance', *Quarterly Essay 12*: Black Ink, Melbourne, 2003.
5 Bellanta, M., *Larrikins, A History*, Penguin Books, Melbourne, 2012.
6 Kingston, B., Reviewing *Larrikins, A History*, *Sydney Morning Herald*, July 21, 2012
7 *Forgotten Australians: A report on Australians who experienced institutional or out-of-home care as children*, Commonwealth of Australia, 2004.
8 Findings of a survey of Queensland Forgotten Australians, RPR Consulting, March 2011.
9 Brett, J. & Moran, A., *Ordinary People's Politics*, Pluto Press, Melbourne, 2006.

Chapter 5

1 Manne, R., 'The war myth that made us', *The Age*, April 25, 2007.
2 http://www.dfat.gov.au/facts/people_culture.html.
3 De Waal, F., *Good Natured, The Origins of Right and Wrong in Humans and Other Animals*, Harvard Universtity Press, Cambridge, 1996.
4 http://australianpolitics.com/political-parties/liberal/the-forgotten-people-robert-menzies-1942-speech.
5 Wilkinson, R. & Pickett, K., *The Spirit Level: Why equality is better for everyone*, Penguin Books, London, 2010.
6 Encel, S., *Equality and Authority*, Tavistock Publications, London, 1970.
7 Horne, D., *The Lucky Country*, Penguin Publishing, Melbourne, 2009
8 Brett, J. & Moran, A., *Ordinary People's Politics*, Pluto Press, Melbourne, 2006.

9 Leigh, A., 'The return of the Australian magnate', *Sydney Morning Herald Opinion*, May 2, 2012.

Chapter 6

1 http://en.wikipedia.org/wiki/Mateship.
2 Lawson, H., *Children of the Bush*, Hard Press, Stockbridge, 2006.
3 Page, J.S., 'Is Mateship a Virtue?', *Australian Journal of Social Issues*, 2002.

Chapter 7

1 Macfarlane, I., The Boyer Lectures, December, 2006.
2 World Economic Outlook Database-October 2012, International Monetary Fund. Accessed 11 October 2012.
3 http://www.smh.com.au/business/australia-the-worlds-second-best-place-to-be-born-study-20121128-2adk0.html#ixzz2Eu3NQ78S.
4 As quoted in 'Local shoppers in "crisis mode"', *Sydney Morning Herald*, May 15, 2012.
5 As quoted in *Managing Prosperity*, Henry, K., Address to the Economic and Social Outlook Conference, Melbourne, November, 2006
6 Irvine, J., 'Unpicking the collective whinge', *Sydney Morning Herald*, May 18, 2012
7 Australia National Report, *Cultural Values Assessment, Australia*, Barrett Values Centre, December, 2009.
8 Devinney, T., Auger, P. & DeSailly, R., *What matters to Australians*, The Anatomy of Civil Societies Research Project, 2012.
9 Boin, A. & Hart, P., *Public Leadership in Times of Crisis: Mission Impossible?*, Challenges of Crisis Management, Sage Publications, California, 2008.
10 'Australia's promise—The next Golden State', *The Economist*, May 26, 2011.

Chapter 8

1 Ketti, D., Managing Boundaries in American Administration: The Collaboration Imperative, Public Administration Review, December 2006
2 O'Flynn, J., The cult of collaboration in public policy. Australian National University National Council of the Institute of Public Administration Australia, 2009
3 Huxham 1996 quoted by Janine O'Flynn, Australian National University. The Cult of Collaboration in Policy. The Australian Journal of Public Administration, vol 68, no 1. pp.112-116, 2009
4 Sennett, R., *Together: The rituals, pleasures and politics of cooperation*, Yale University Press, New Haven, 2012.
5 Kearney, G., Play nice, Fast thinking, ETN-COM on behalf of The Innovation Xchange, Spring, 2008.
6 Rosemary O'Leary. The skill set of the successful collaborator. Public Administration Review, Vol. xx, 2012

Chapter 9

1 Howard, J., 'Fair Australia', one of a series of Headland speeches given to the ACOSS Congress 1995
2 Sheridan, S.J., 'Farewell Message', http://blog.getup.org.au/2011/07/28/a-message-from-simon, 2012.
3 Costello, T., as quoted in the Good Weekend, July 2012.

Chapter 10

1 Diamond, J., http://www.juliediamond.net/blog/underestimating-our-own-power/
2 Mindell, A., *Sitting in the Fire: Large Group Transformation using Conflict & Diversity*, Lao Tse Press, Portland, 1995.

Chapter 11

1 Reed, B., An Exploration of Role, The Grubb Institute, London, 2006
2 Sheridan, S.J., 'Farewell Message', *The National Times*, November 15, 2009
3 Reed, B., An Exploration of Role, The Grubb Institute, London, 2006.
4 Block, P., *Community: The structure of belonging*, Barrett Koehler Publisher, San Francisco, 2008.
5 Heifetz, R., Linsky, M., Grashow, A., *Practice of Adpative Leadership: Tools and Tactics for Changing Your Organization and the World*, Harvard University Press, Cambridge, 2009.
6 Reed, B., An Exploration of Role, The Grubb Institute, London, 2006.

Chapter 12

1 Fitzsimmons, C., 'How to get ahead at work', *Australian Financial Review*, November, 2012
2 Weiss, L., True collaboration embraces conflict, Management Innovation Exchange, 2011

3 Lewis, M., *Inside the NO: Five Steps to Decisions That Last*, Johannesburg, Self published, 2008.
4 Siver, S., Deep Democracy: Multidimensional Process-Oriented Leadership, from *The Handbook for working with difficult groups*, Jossey-Bass, San Fransisco, 2010
5 Heifetz, R., Linsky, M., Grashow, A., *Practice of Adpative Leadership: Tools and Tactics for Changing Your Organization and the World*, Harvard University Press, Cambridge, 2009.
6 Kelly, P., *The End of Certainty*, Allen & Unwin, Sydney, 1994.
7 Lewis, M., *Inside the NO: Five steps to decisions that last*, self-published, Johannesburg, 2008.
8 Parker, P., http://priya-parker.com/blog/what-do-conflict-innovation-have-in-common

Chapter 13

1 Milliken, F. J., Morrison, E. W., 'Speaking Up, Remaining Silent: The Dynamics of Voice and Silence in Organizations', Journal of Management Studies, Volume 40, Issue 6, September 2003
2 Heifetz, R., *Leadership Without Eeasy Answers*, Cambridge, Harvard University Press, 1998.

Chapter 15

1 Deveson, A., *Resilience*, Allen & Unwin, Sydney, 2003.
2 Nohria, N., Khurana, R., *Handbook of Leadership Theory and Practice*, Harvard University Press, Cambridge, 2010.
3 Aigner, G., *Leadership Beyond Good Intentions*, Allen & Unwin, Sydney, 2011.

Chapter 16

1 Malouf, D., 'Made in England: Australia's British Inheritance', *Quarterly Essay 12*: Black Ink, Melbourne, 2003.

INDEX

accountability 175
adaptive challenges 18–21
　collaboration and 91
　conflict 150
adversity and prosperity paradox
　　74–84
　implications 80–2
　opportunities 82–4
Amin, Idi xx
Anatomy of Civil Societies
　　Research Project
　What Matters to Australians
　　Report 2012 80
anti-authority and authority-
　　dependent paradox 31–46,
　　107, 152–3, 177
　implications 43–4
　opportunities of 45–6
Anzac Day 63
appreciation and compassion
　　196–7
Australia
　asylum-seekers 18, 20, 81, 88
　Australian cringe 105–6
　battlers 74–6
　classlessness 50–2
　colonial dependence 31–3
　diversity 88
　divisive issues 20
　educational funding 69–70
　egalitarian and hierarchical
　　paradox 47–59
　equality 52–5
　exercise of leadership in 9–10

'fair go' 48, 52, 55
future development 211–12
Indigenous people xxiii–xxiv,
　　33, 40–1, 74, 109, 115, 116,
　　118–19
larrikinism 37–9
leadership mobility 58
mateship 60
media sector 19
natural disasters 75
new leadership story 210–13
prosperity 76–8
rank sensitivity 55–6
social mobility 58
space and distance benefit
　　12–13
stories of and influences on
　　leadership xxiii–xxiv
thinking and practice of
　　leadership xv–xvii, xxi–xxii
UK, relationship with 34–6
US, relationship with 35
Australian Charities Fund 11
Australian Commonwealth Court
　　of Conciliation and
　　Arbitration 39
Australian economy xiv
　adversity or prosperity 74–84
Australian flag 63
'The Australian Settlement' 32–3
authority 15–17, 98
　adaptive role 140, 182–4
　attack or compliance, reverting
　　to 198–9

INDEX

Australian perceptions 31–46
balanced relationship with 177–8
blinkered view by 179
bringing forward the 'no' 166–7
'broker of difference' 165
change and 182–3
constraints 175, 190
context story 186
corrupt or dangerous 180–1
dependence on 36, 152–3
distinction from leadership 15–17
distraction, vulnerability to 179–80
doing business with 175–99
early experience of 186–7
enticement/seduction of 198
flaws 188
functions 15–16, 139–40, 182–3
higher level of 185–6
holding environment, part of 181
holding the conflict 168–71
implications of paradox 43–4
kneejerk responses 176
larrikins and 37–9
mistrust of 39–43
narrative 184–7
personal story 178, 190, 200–1
protecting the 'no' 167–8
resource, as 181–2
rewriting narrative 187–8
role 16–17, 138–40, 153–4, 165, 166–73, 182–3, 189
stories about 184–7
system story 186–7
teacher, as 199
technical role 140
timing and capacity 190–1
transience 188
understanding and practice of different roles 140–4
universal story 185–6
working with 178–84
world story 184–5

Barrett Values Centre 78–9
Behrendt, Larissa 67, 206–7
Bligh, Anna 141
Block, Peter 137
Boehm, Christopher 49
Boston Consulting Group 77
Bouazizi, Mohammed xix
boys' club 63, 66
Brett, Judith
    Ordinary People's Politics 45
Brooks, Rebekah 10–11

carbon pricing, introduction of 20–1
Carnival Australia 19
change see also leading across difference
    below, generated from 182
    challenges and opportunities 87–8

clear and compelling purpose 102
organisations 19–20, 54, 63–4
resistance to 121–2
systems and change 19–20, 182–4
threat interpretation 183
Child Migrants Programme 41
child sexual abuse 42
climate change 20, 88
collaboration 89–90 see also holding environment
adaptive challenge 91
commitment 95–6
competition 93–4
control 94–5
interpersonal skills 96–7
leading across difference 89–90, 92
raised expectations 90–1
'seduction' of 902
technical challenges 91
three Cs of collaborating 92–6
uncertainty 92
when required 91
collective purpose 102–5
action from guilt or privilege 103
call to action 102–5
self-interest 103–4
where and why questions 102–6
commitment and collaboration 95–6

community sector 134
competition 93
competition and collaboration 93–4
competition and mateship 68–70
implications 70–2
opportunities 72–3
complacency 78–80
conflict 149–74
anti-authority 153–4
Australia and 152–6
avoiding 156–7
causes 150–1
cult of 'yes' 156–7
dependence on authority 152–3
egalitarian values 155–6
'holding environment' 160–4 see also holding environment
importance of 173–4
innovation, importance for 156–8
loss of 'no' 157–8
productive 150–2, 159–60, 168–71
relational implications 154–5
Constitution referendum 1999 61–2
'consumerisation of followers' 6
consumerism 69
control and collaboration 94–5
Costello, Tim 104–5
crisis 80–1, 103, 141
addiction to 78–80

INDEX

catalyst for change 103
  leadership 75–6
Cronulla Beach riots 63
Curtin, John 35
cynicism 37, 79, 106

Dalai Lama 115–16
'deep democracy' 166
dependency
  comfort and lure of 34–5
  force of 31–4
  trust and 35–7
direction through life 15–16
diversity of difference 88–9
doing business with authority
    175–99
  groundwork 189–93
  mutuality of need 177
  skills and techniques 193–7
  traps 197–9
Dowler, Milly 10

The Economist 76, 77
egalitarian societies 49–50
egalitarian values 155–6
egalitarianism and hierarchical
    paradox 47–59
  opportunities 57–9
  preoccupation with the middle
    50–2, 56–7
  rank 55–6
Egypt xix
employment rate 76
Encel, Sol 53

entropy 78–9
equality 197–8
ethics 11
expectations xiii, 7
  political 14–15

failures of leadership 11
Faine, Jon 4
family as function of authority
    15–16
Fitzgerald, Robert 212
forced adoption policies 41
'Forgotten Australians' 41–2

Gaddafi, Muammar xx
Gallop, Geoff xvi, 89
GetUp 77, 139
Gbagbo, President Laurent xix
GDP 76, 77
gender and leadership 27–8
Gillard government 20–1, 51
Gillard, Julia 137
global financial crisis 18, 79, 115
Goodstart Early Learning Centre
    11
government sector
  collaboration 93, 94–5
governments, Australian attitudes
    to 33
groundwork for leadership
    189–93
  awareness of personal story 190
  needs and constraints upon
    authority 190

owning problems 193
realistic progress, recognising 191–2
reputation, understanding 192
timing and capacity 190–1
understanding and owning our power and rank 192–3
unmet demands 191–2
growth 149–74
   conflict as signal of 150–1
   importance of 173–4

Harvester Judgement 39
Hawke, Bob 161
Hawke government 161
Heifetz, Ronald 184
HiCAps 127
hierarchy, growth in 53–4
Higgins, Henry B. 39
holding environment 160–4, 171
   authority as part of 181
   clear authority and sufficient structure 162
   diversity of participants 164
   existing culture 163
   facilitation 163
   familiarity with adaptive work 164
   physical environment 162–3
   reputation and relationships 163
   time as tool 163–4
   trust of authority 164
   urgency 164

honeymoon period for new leaders 5
Horne, Donald 9
'Howard battlers' 51
Howard government 39
Howard, John 50, 51, 60, 61
Human Development Index 76
Hutchinson, Greg 11

Indigenous people
   assimilation policies 40
   dependence positioning 33
   dispossession impact 74
   gap in social and health well-being 109
   psychological rank 115, 118–19
   spiritual rank 116
   Stolen Generation 40–1
   wisdom of leadership xiv
   working with non-Indigenous people xxiii
individualism 69
informality 60
innovation 88, 98, 149–74
   authority, role of 165–73
   barriers to 93–6
   bringing forward the 'no' 166–7
   dependence on authority 152–3
   emotional and psychological commitment 150
   facilitating the 'no' 165–73
   holding environment 160–4 see also holding environment

importance of conflict 156–8, 159, 173–4
promoting, important step in 172–3
interpersonal skills 96–7
IPSOS Mori and Catalyst Research 154
Ivory Coast xix

Japan xx
'jasmine revolution' xix
Jumbunna Indigenous House of Learning 67

Keating, Paul 161
Kelly, Paul 32
Kingston, Beverley 38
knowledge is power attitude 95

larrikinism 37–9, 153
Lawson, Henry 62
leaders 22–3
  accountability 175
  archetypal 184–5
  constraints 175, 190
  groundwork 189–93
  role as 127
  skills and techniques 193–7
  world story 184–5
leadership
  adaptive 18–21
  authority, distinction 15–17
  'being of' 202–4
  challenges xiv, xviii
  common elements 27–8
  cost of 203
  crisis and 75–6
  culture of complaint xvi, xviii, 3–6, 12
  democratisation of xx
  effective xvii, 8
  fantasy 6–9
  forms of 21–2
  functions 21–2
  Indigenous xxiv, 206–7
  letting go 207–9
  masculine models 27–8
  national elements 28
  perceptions of 5–6
  personal sustainability 203–4
  purpose xiv
  purposeful xvi–xviii
  resilience, quality of 203–4
  role, authority and 138–40
  sports, in 9–10
  superhuman qualities 8
  surviving and thriving 204–7
  technical challenges 17–18
  traditional concept xiii, xxi
  vision xvii–xviii, 99–102
  world hope for xvii–xx, 6–7
leading across difference 87–9, 152
  collaboration 89–90
  collective purpose 97, 102–5
  interpersonal skills 96–7
  power, rank and authority 97
  requirements 96–8

roles 97–8, 125–48
Lewis, Myrna 166
Libya xx
lightning rod, becoming 198
LinkedIn 154
loss minimisation 195
loyalty 63

Macfarlane, Ian 76
Malouf, David 36
management 17, 176
managing-up 176
masculine leadership models 27–8
mateship 60–2
   competition as shadow side of 68–70
   dynamics 63, 64, 71
   exclusion from 67–8
   function of 63
   implications of competition and 70–2
   male focus 65–6, 68
   military associations 66
   purpose 67
   relational culture 62–5
   women and 66, 67–8
measurements and feedback mechanisms 6
Menzies, Robert 50–1
meta-communication 193–5

Mindell, Arnold 110, 166
modelling boundaries 196
Mornings 4
Mubarak, Hosni xix
Mugabe, Robert xx
Murdoch, Rupert 10–11
Murray, Les 61–2

National Economic Summit 161
natural disasters 75
negativity 4–5
News International 10–11
News of the World 10–11

OECD 69
order and discipline 16
organisations and change 19–20, 54, 63–4
organisations and factions 93
organisations and roles 127–8
Ouattara, Alassane xix

paradoxes of Australian leadership
   adversity and prosperity 74–84
   anti-authority and authority-dependent 31–46, 107, 152–3, 177
   egalitarian and hierarchical 47–59

leading across difference 87–8, 96–8
patterns of practice 28–30
relational and competitive 60–73
partnering with authority 197–8
patriotism 63
pessimism 78
Pew Research 5
phone hacking scandal 10–11
Pickett, Kate
'Spirit Level' study 52, 58
political expectations 14–15
polls 6
power, rank and authority 107–24
  informal power 175
  positional and social power 176
  power and grace 122–3
  power structures xi, 4–5, 10–12, 37, 94–5
  rank, understanding 109–16 see also rank
  underdog form of power 107–8
  understanding and owning 192–3
  using power 109, 134–5
  victims and tyrants 108
Process Orientated Psychology 110
Productivity Commission 83
prosperity in Australia 76–8
protective function of family 16

Queensland floods 75

rank
  awareness of privilege 117–19
  battle for 121–2
  change resistance 121–2
  class, distinction 110
  conflict, causes of 116–17
  context 110–11, 114
  definition 109
  earned 109
  factional 193
  hiding 116
  identification and categorisation 110
  Indigenous people 115, 116, 118–19
  low transferability 114
  owning or not owning 116–20
  positional 111–12, 114
  psychological 114–15
  sensitivity 55–6, 1117
  social 112–13
  spiritual 114, 115–16
  types 111–16
  understanding 109–16
  unearned 109, 112–13, 114
  use for benefit of others 117–18
Reed, Bruce 135–6, 142
relational and competitive paradox 60–73, 154
  implications 70–2
  opportunities 72–3
republicanism 34–5
Reserve Bank 76
roles 97–8

action with authenticity 140–4
archetypal 126
Australian leadership 144–5
authority, leadership and 138–40
authority, of see authority
clarity of 137–8
context 126, 131–2
descriptions 125–6
expectations and competing needs 126
finding 142
formal 126
identity-based 128–9
impacts on 130–8
informal 126, 127
invisible context 132
leader, as 127
leverage of 125–48
making 142–3
personal context 132
personal relationships 135–6
resilience and safety 136–8
self and, distinction 137
taking up 127, 130, 143
understanding of own role 125–30
using power with purpose 134–5
visible context 131
whole-system 128
Rudd government 51
Rudd, Kevin xvi, 39, 40

Sennett, Richard
  Together 94
7.30 Report 137
Sheikh, Simon 77, 139
Sherry, Ann 19
Shimizu, President Masataka xx
skills and techniques 193–7
skin in the game 94
Social Leadership Australia (SLA) ix, xiii, xxii–xxiv, 83, 176, 183, 197
social media xix, xx
society
  adaptive challenges 18–21
  response to technical challenges 17–18
Southern Cross 63
sport 9–10, 68
State of Origin 68
Stolen Generation 40–1
support for authority's functions 195–6
systems and change 19–20
  challenge to become more adaptive 182–4

'tall-poppy syndrome' 49
Taylor, Doug 92, 144
technical challenges 17–18
  collaboration and 91
TEPCO xx
Terry, Simon 127
Tingle, Laura 33
Tunisia xix

Ullman, Chris 137
unemployment rate 76
United Nations 76
United Way 92, 144
University of Technology 67

values 18, 20, 21, 30, 43, 53, 55,
　　57–8, 61, 63–5, 67, 89, 93–4,
　　117, 141, 151–2
　egalitarian 155–6
　national assessment 78–9
　tension between individual and
　　collective 69–70
Victorian bushfires 75
vision xvii–xix, 99–102
　Australian leadership and global
　　impact 100–2
　positive social impact of
　　leadership 99
　responsibility for Australian
　　leadership 99–100
　shared 101
voter research 6

Weiss, Leigh 156
What Matters to Australians
　Report 2012 80
Wikileaks xix
Wilkinson, Richard 53
　'Spirit Level' study 52, 58
WorkChoices 39
workplace relationships 61
World Vision Australia 104